THEY NEVER LEFT ME

Praise for *They Never Left Me*

"A brilliant book and an amazing work.

"At the end of *They Never Left Me* Evelyn states that, 'Writing a memoir in your ninth decade has its limitations.' Of course. But it also enhances the scope of her vision. She captures the fullness of a life well lived despite the tragic upheavals and challenges of the Shoah, the catastrophe known as the Holocaust.

"Hers was a young life marked by close calls, split-second decisions, avoiding Jew-hunters (including Nazis and enthusiastic collaborators)—and mastering the art of silence. Throughout, Evelyn retained a measure of faith and hope. How is that possible?

"Elie Wiesel commented on hope. 'Jews have every reason to despair. But we cannot. We must not. For we are commanded to hope.'

"Evelyn has provided a legacy of memory for her children, grandchildren and for us all. In that act alone, resides the possibility of hope."

DR. ROBERT KRELL, CM, MD | Child Holocaust survivor; emeritus professor of psychiatry, University of British Columbia and founding president of the Vancouver Holocaust Education Centre

"Meet the miraculous, authentic voice of a little Jewish girl whose mother and grandmother's grit and indomitable love refused to let her become another statistic of the Nazi mass murderers. Three generations of Jewish women who would survive against all odds. A riveting story.

RABBI ABRAHAM COOPER | Simon Wiesenthal Center, Associate Dean & Global Social Action Director

"Evelyn's story is one not only of survival but one that showcases the importance of hope during the darkest times.

"As the late Rabbi Lord Jonathan Sacks taught, 'Optimism and hope are not the same. Optimism is the belief that the world is changing for the better; hope is the belief that, together, we can make the world better. Optimism is a passive virtue, hope an active one. It needs no courage to be an optimist, but it takes a great deal of courage to hope.'

"Young Evelyn had great courage, surviving unimaginable horrors and building a life in Canada. Her story is one that must inspire all who cherish life and liberty. As links in a chain, it is a call to action: to remember our story; reclaim all that has been weaponized to demonize, delegitimize, and apply double standards against our people, normalizing an ever-mutating lethal hate; and to renew the pledge of 'never again,' at a time that the Holocaust itself has been hijacked and inverted to justify genocidal intent, 'again and again.'"

MICHAL COTLER-WUNSH | Former Member of Knesset
Israel's Special Envoy for Combatting Antisemitism

"The idyllic start of Ewa's life, surrounded by a large and loving family and community, juxtaposes horrifically with the abrupt cataclysm of history that would follow. The survival of three generations of women in the forests of eastern Europe is a monument to human resolve and resilience. *They Never Left Me* is a momentous contribution to the literature of the Holocaust."

PAT JOHNSON | Journalist
Jewish Independent Vancouver

They Never Left Me

A HOLOCAUST MEMOIR OF MATERNAL COURAGE AND TRIUMPH

EVELYN KAHN
WITH HODIE KAHN

RONSDALE

RONSDALE PRESS
125A – 1030 Denman Street, Vancouver, B.C. Canada V6G 2M6
www.ronsdalepress.com

Cover and book design: Barbi Braude
Digital collage and map illustrations: Barbi Braude
Editor: Robyn So
Proofreader: Kelly Laycock
Graphic legend chapter introductions: Evelyn Kahn's handwriting

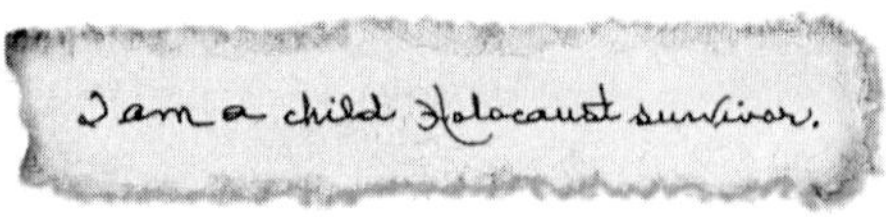

Ronsdale Press wishes to thank the following for their support of its publishing program: the Canada Council for the Arts, the Government of Canada, the British Columbia Arts Council, and the Province of British Columbia through the British Columbia Book Publishing Tax Credit program.

Library and Archives Canada Cataloguing in Publication

Title: They never left me : a Holocaust memoir of maternal courage and triumph | Evelyn Kahn and Hodie Kahn.
Names: Kahn, Evelyn, author. | Kahn, Hodie, author.
Description: Includes bibliographical references.
Identifiers: Canadiana (print) 20250230127 | Canadiana (ebook) 20250230143 | ISBN 9781553807322 (softcover) | ISBN 9781553807339 (EPUB)
Subjects: LCSH: Kahn, Evelyn—Childhood and youth. | LCSH: Mothers and daughters—Biography. | LCSH: Holocaust, Jewish (1939-1945)—Personal narratives. | LCSH: Holocaust survivors—Poland—Biography. | LCSH: Holocaust survivors—Belarus—Biography. | LCSH: Jewish children in the Holocaust—Poland—Biography. | LCSH: Jewish children in the Holocaust—Belarus—Biography. | LCGFT: Personal narratives.
Classification: LCC DS134.72.K34 A3 2025 | DDC 940.53/18092—dc23

At Ronsdale Press we are committed to protecting the environment. To this end we are working with Canopy and printers to phase out our use of paper produced from ancient forests. This book is one step towards that goal.

Printed in Canad

This book is dedicated to the souls who gave me life.

Moshe Landsman *z"l*,[1] beloved Papa

Basia ("Bashke") Landsman *z"l*, beloved Mama

Hoda Schuster *z"l*, my "kluge" (wise) grandmother

Riva ("Rivke") Joselewitz *z"l*, my dear aunt

And to all of those who didn't live to tell their own stories—
my extended family, my friends,
and every voice silenced by the Shoah.

I will honour your memories forever.

1. *z"l* is an abbreviation for *zichorno livracha* (Hebrew, masc.) or *zichorona livracha* (Hebrew, fem.), meaning "of blessed memory."

Memory is my story,
the past that made me who I am,
of whose legacy I am the guardian
for the sake of generations
yet to come.

Without memory,
there is no identity,
and without identity,
we are mere dust
on the surface of infinity.

Rabbi Lord Jonathan Sacks *zt"l*,[1]
Morality: Restoring the Common Good in Divided Times

1. *zt"l* is an abbreviation for *zecher tzaddik livracha*, meaning "May the memory of the righteous one be a blessing."

Contents

Author's Note

I always feel blessed to have survived. I still wonder how I did. Divine providence, good fortune and the unwavering courage of others—certainly. But I believe the quiet, steady presence of profound faith, nurtured in me from the time I was born, also played a critical role. Because faith is hope. Even in the bleakest moments of the Holocaust, as the Nazis stole everything—including the lives of beloved family members—they never managed to steal that. Faith shaped the chaos of my life and offered meaning beyond mere survival.

As Viktor Frankl eloquently wrote in *Man's Search for Meaning*, "The primary human drive is not pleasure but the pursuit of what we find meaningful." For me, that meaning was faith and hope—and love.

For a long time, I believed my story did not matter as much as those of adult survivors, that it did not carry the same weight. Their stories felt so detailed, so devastating—so large. Mine, by comparison, felt small. More passive observer than active participant, I was not even sure how I could ever articulate it. My family never spoke about the Holocaust after the war, so neither did I. We lived in the present. Silence was its own form of survival.

A psychiatrist I saw briefly in my seventies gently challenged that silence. He told me that telling my story was crucial—especially for my children. But between marriage, raising a family and caring for others, there was little time left for myself. Writing down my memories felt simply too difficult.

AUTHOR'S NOTE

It wasn't until after the passing of my beloved husband, Leon Kahn *z"l*, in 2003 that I finally had the space to begin.

The Holocaust never left me, but capturing it on paper meant retrieving memories buried deep in the corners of my soul. It meant confronting not only the trauma and grief of that time, but also all the sorrows that followed.

So I write now, knowing that I must. I am in the twilight of my life on Earth, and my time here is waning.

My story is uncommon, even rare. It is the story of three generations of women survivors—my grandmother Hoda, my mother Basia and my aunt Rivke. Three women who walked through hell and not only survived, but did so with their humanity and faith intact. They protected me unconditionally, again and again, risking their lives so that I might live. It is a story of resilience and courage. It is about loyalty, sacrifice and the enduring power of love for others over love of self. And it is about the triumph of the spirit over those who sought to crush it.

This story is not just mine. It is also theirs.

I write this memoir to honour the indomitable women who taught me to trust in God even when the world fell apart—who showed me how to grow from pain and how to carry both grief and joy in the same heart. I write it to honour my gentle beloved father, Moshe *z"l*, who laid the foundation of my faith in the precious, but too brief, time we shared. How blessed I am that their blood runs in my veins.

I am their legacy.

I never thought this memoir would be anything but my own legacy. But to my deep dismay, I fear it is not. As I began writing and drew closer to completing it, the distant echo of anti-Semitism began to loom again—growing into an ominous drumbeat, portending both the threat and reality of a new Holocaust.

If those who forget history are destined to repeat it, then those who remember it should not have to relive it.

So I close with a prayer that the Holocaust I lived through—and my story—be the last one.

New York
Bremerhaven
Berlin
GERMANY
POLAND
LITHUANIA
BELARU
Vilna
Eishyshok
Lida
PUSZCZA
LIPICHANSKA
Zhetel
Ludzichy
Lodz
Jordanbad
Singen
Gailingen
Landsberg

Prologue

Rounded up before dawn, we had been standing in the crowded marketplace for hours, along with hundreds of other Jews from the Zhetel ghetto. Armed Nazi SS Einsatzgruppen and Belorussian auxiliary police surrounded us.

Finally, our attention shifted to an SS officer at the centre of the square as he began to read out names from a prepared list in his hands. I could hear screaming and crying all around me as each name was called. One by one, 119 men—and one lone woman—were separated from their families and loaded onto open-back military transport trucks parked at the edge of the square.

An uneasy quiet descended as the trucks pulled away. Perhaps it was over. Perhaps we would be allowed to go home. Then, before I fully understood what was happening, my father lifted me into his arms. Holding me tightly against him, he told me he had to go.

"Mayn tayere kind, du bist mayn osher (My dearest child, you are my treasure)," he said, kissing me on my forehead before gently setting me down next to my weeping mother.

He was already walking away as my farewell left my lips.

"Tayere Papa, kum tsurik tsu unz (Dearest Papa, come back to us)!"

And then he was gone.

LITHUANIA
BELARUS
Vilna
Eishyshok
Lida
Zhetel
PUSZCZA
LIPICHANSKA
Ludzichy

PART ONE
Childhood

Eishyshok

May 1933 – September 1939

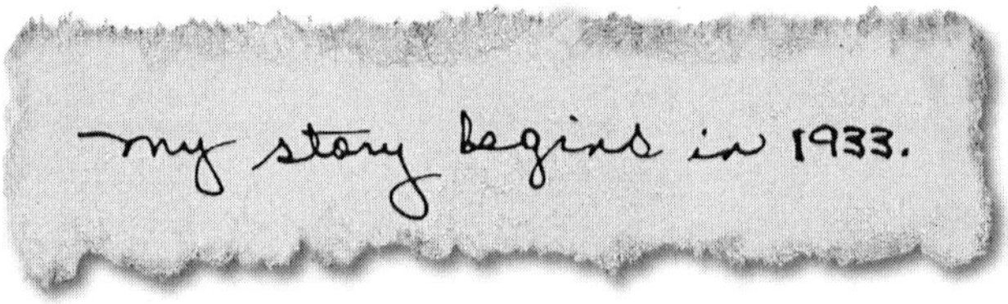

It was a beautiful spring day that year when Moshe and Basia Landsman set out from their *shtetl* of Eishyshok,[1] on the Polish-Lithuanian border, to visit relatives in the larger nearby city of Vilna. The couple had been married for barely a year, and Basia, (Bashke to her family) was pregnant. I imagine them savouring a last opportunity to enjoy time together as a twosome. A little holiday to take in Vilna's arts and culture, stroll along the city's beautiful tree-lined avenues, and riverfront promenades and spend time with Moshe's brother and his family.

Moshe and Basia Landsman, wedding portrait, Eishyshok, July 5, 1932.
COURTESY OF EVELYN KAHN

It was a good plan. But, as the saying goes, "Man plans and God laughs."

I am not sure how far Moshe and Basia got into their trip before God needed a good chuckle. Basia went into premature labour and was rushed to hospital. My breech presentation did

1. Because of the region's shifting borders and multilingual history, many place names appear in different forms depending on the language and the time period. Throughout this memoir many names are transliterated from Yiddish, reflecting the way these towns and regions were known to the author and her community at the time the events occurred. Please refer to the table of Geographic Names and Regional Spellings at the end of the book for further information.

not make my entry into this world easy for either one of us. I finally arrived at 3:02 a.m. on Wednesday, May 17, scrunched and swollen, with a face I was later told resembled a squashed tomato. My parents named me Ewa (Eve, pronounced Eva in Polish and Chava in Hebrew) after Moshe's mother, who had passed away four months earlier. My parents were now officially Papa and Mama.

Eishyshok

Eishyshok was one of the oldest Jewish communities in Lithuania, tracing its roots back to the mid-eleventh century. Pre–World War II, it was home to thirty-five hundred Jews, who made up nearly 75% of the local population. There were three prayer houses; several schools; cultural, sports and Zionist clubs; a library; children's camps; live theatre; and even a cinema. Located near the southeastern border with Belarus, the town's sovereignty shifted several times due to geopolitical conflicts. During the twentieth century alone, the town fell under the control of Lithuania, Russia, Poland, Nazi Germany and the Soviet Union. During the interwar period (1922–1939), Eishyshok was part of Poland. Today it is known as Eišiškės, Lithuania. Only a few dozen of its Jews survived the Holocaust. There are no Jews left in Eishyshok today.

My mother's postpartum recovery was complicated and prolonged, as she developed a life-threatening thrombosis during my delivery that travelled from her abdomen to her leg. A wonderful surgeon saved Basia's life, but the thrombosis resulted in an open ulcer on the shin of her left leg. She always wore a bandage over the wound and it was not until I was older that I was permitted to see it. I would watch her apply different ointments, covering the ulcer with gauze compresses and then wrapping a tensor bandage around her lower leg to keep the dressing in place.

I believe my parents stayed in Vilna for several weeks after I was born. They eventually returned home to Eishyshok, where

Basia convalesced for an entire year. She was so weak during the early postpartum months that she was only able to hold me long enough to nurse me. Thankfully, her mother, Hoda, whom I called Bobe (grandmother), and her youngest sister, Riva, whom we called Rivke, lived with us and were able to care for me until my mother regained her strength.

I was the light of my parents' lives. As far as they were concerned, their little newborn was a vision of uncompromising perfection. Mama looked past my misshapen and puffy countenance and saw a beauty. Papa saw a princess. Some of Basia's friends, on the other hand, saw a baby with the proverbial face only a mother (or father) could love. My mother once recounted to me that shortly after she returned from Vilna a couple of her friends stopped by to greet her newborn. After taking a look at me, one of the women could not hold back and blurted, "How can you love such an ugly baby?" Basia was incensed and profoundly hurt but too polite to respond in the moment. However, she never forgot the insult and neither woman was ever invited back. My mother never had an opportunity to repair the relationships. Both women perished in the Holocaust.

By my first birthday all visible signs of the trauma of my birth had disappeared. I was, according to Basia's admittedly prejudiced eyes, a vision of angelic loveliness and an aristocratically beautiful little girl, a perfect blend of the best of Mama and Papa.

Basia's features suggested some long-ago genetic mix of Spanish and Mediterranean ancestry. She had an oval face, beautiful dark eyes and hair, an olive complexion and naturally rosy cheeks that never needed blush. Tall and long-legged, Basia had beautiful posture and wore her clothes with ease. I did not inherit my mother's height, topping out at 5 feet, 3 inches. But I must have inherited her posture, as I am often told I look taller than I am. My mother was always smartly dressed. For work she favoured fine wool or silk dresses in black, with pinafores and white blouses with starched white collars and stiff silk cuffs called *manchettes*. I can still see them peeking out from the sleeves of her coat.

Moshe had a light complexion, blue eyes, wavy light brown hair, broad shoulders and a medium build. That is a good description of me too, only my hair was closer to dark blond as a child. (It became decidedly darker as I got older, and then magically blond again when I got even older.) I know my mother was 5 feet, 8 inches tall, so my best guess is that Papa was probably closer to 5 feet, 7 inches, as I remember him being slightly shorter than Mama. He was very dapper, always neat and well dressed. He wore suits of houndstooth checks, small plaids and salt and pepper tweeds. A vest and grey fedora completed his ensembles. In later life I would watch movies with British actors and be struck by how much those very urbane gentlemen reminded me of Papa.

I was my father's most precious possession. He took no chances safeguarding his priceless treasure, including having Mama indulge his superstitions by putting a *bendl* around my tiny wrist. It was a thin piece of red-coloured string that was believed to protect the wearer from the *ayin hara*, the evil eye. The sun rose and set with my name on Papa's lips. He was my Papa and I was his Chavale. I can still feel him beside me, walking together hand in hand.

Moshe was born in 1905 to Shlomo and Chava Landsman in the large Black Sea port city of Odessa, Ukraine. Papa had one brother, Henoch, who was two years younger. Odessa was then under Soviet control, so both brothers were educated in Russian. I believe Moshe finished high school in Odessa before the family moved to Podbrodze, in Lithuania, about fifty kilometres northeast of Vilna.

Moshe was instructed in Jewish and secular studies and later became an accountant by profession. He worked for several businesses in Eishyshok and volunteered his professional skills with community organizations, including the Free Loan Society, which extended economic assistance to those in need, and as secretary of the *va'ad*, the Jewish community council, which helped make decisions on matters such as charity distribution, communal services and dispute resolutions. My father spoke five languages fluently: Yiddish, Hebrew, Russian, Polish and German, and he studied the burgeoning international language of Esperanto.

I was captivated on weekday mornings watching my father ready himself for his traditional morning prayers and special ritual practices. He started by saying a blessing as he draped himself in his *tallit*, his prayer shawl. Then he put on his *tefillin*, his phylacteries, a set of two small black leather boxes containing verses from the Torah, bound to the arm and forehead with leather straps. Papa would say a blessing and gently kiss one little black box, slide it onto his left arm up to his bicep and then wrap the box's single leather strap around his arm seven times. He would then say another blessing and take the second box and place it just above his hairline on his forehead, letting both straps of that box hang down behind his head. He finished the ritual by rewrapping the strap on his arm in an intricate weave through the fingers of his left hand. When everything was in order, he began to pray, swaying gently from side to side. I loved to watch as he swayed and prayed. It was beautiful and calming.

Papa taught me how to start my day with the morning ritual of *negel vasser* (nail water), rinsing our hands, he explained, of any impurities (and evil spirits). The ritual was also performed before praying or studying Torah, and Papa showed me how to pour water three times over each hand, alternating them, with the special two-handled washing cup. After my hands were rinsed, I said the *Modeh Ani* (I Am Thankful), a prayer to express my gratitude to God for returning my soul to my body. In the evenings, my father read Yiddish nursery rhymes to me and then told me about all the wonderful things we would do together during the week, before leading me in saying the bedtime *Shema* prayer before I went to sleep, to ask God to watch over my soul through the night.

Moshe was traditional but also very much a part of the modern world. He listened regularly to the radio and read newspapers, no doubt to stay up on politics and current events. I have a particularly strong memory of Papa wearing a black armband, which I believe now must have commemorated the anniversary of the death of Polish statesman Marshal Józef Piłsudski, who believed in ethnic equality for all Poles, including Jews.

My sense is that my worldly father would have preferred to live in Vilna, both for its sophistication and to be near Henoch, his brother and only sibling.

Henoch was the head accountant for a large firm there and lived a very gracious lifestyle with his wife, Rachil (Rachel), and their only child, Shlomo Leib (who we affectionately called Lolek). These were the relatives my mother and father were visiting when my mother went into labour with me. They lived in a lovely apartment on

Zawalna Street. I was very impressed by the refinement and furnishings of their home and still recall the table in their house covered with a beautiful damask tablecloth upon which were laid wonderful delicacies that I never saw in Eishyshok.

Rachil was from a wealthy family. She was very refined and always beautifully dressed. I have an especially vivid memory of her in a chic, belted, burgundy-coloured leather trench coat, which she wore with a beautiful hat. Lolek was around two years older than me. Very cute, with blond hair and blue eyes, my cousin was my knight in shining armour. He loved taking me around town to buy me sweets and ice cream. Aunt Rachil dressed him in stylish breeches, with knee-high textured socks and fine shoes.

Vilna

Vilna, sixty kilometres north and due east of Eishyshok, was a key hub of spiritual and cultural life for Eastern European Jewry before World War II. The "Jerusalem of Lithuania" was filled with more than a hundred synagogues, as well as many religious, scientific and secular educational institutions. There were theatres, museums, libraries and publishing houses; scores of gifted and notable rabbis and Talmudic scholars, including the renowned Rabbi Elijah ben Solomon Zalman known as the Vilna Gaon (Hebrew for "genius"), and creatives, and contemporary thinkers across the political spectrum. Like Eishsyhok, Vilna's shifting sovereignty was reflected in the diversity of the local population of Jews, Poles, Belorussians and Russians. It is known today as Vilnius and is the capital of Lithuania. An estimated fifty-five thousand Jews lived in Vilna before the war, making up approximately 30% of the population. Only a few thousand survived the Holocaust.

Unfortunately, the war put a bitter end to our time together. Henoch, Rachil and Lolek were among the Vilna Jews massacred in the Ponary Forest in the summer of 1941. Had my father moved us to

Vilna, as I believe he wished, our fate would likely have been the same. But my father knew how important it was for Basia to be close to her family for both emotional and economic support. My mother's conscience would not allow her to abandon her mother. Papa's devotion to Mama meant she would not have to.

Basia had strong roots in Eishyshok. Her father, Rav Yosef Schuster, and his family had been there for generations. He was one of four children of Chaim and Sarah Schuster and their only son. His three sisters, Guta Leah, Basia Bayle and Chasya, all immigrated to the United States between the turn of the century and World War I. Rav Yosef remained in Europe.

Rav Yosef Schuster, Eishyshok, c. 1880s.
COURTESY OF EVELYN KAHN

Basia's mother Hoda was born on March 27, 1879, in Pumpyan, a small town in central northeastern Lithuania, then part of the Russian Empire. The eldest of Yanekl and Rivke Kats's five children, she was followed by Elka Mirka, Zundel Leyb (Louis), Peysakh Leizer and Chava Sora. Her sisters moved to Estonia and Latvia after they married, and Hoda lost contact with them. Her brothers immigrated to South Africa in the early 1900s, joining a large wave of Lithuanian Jews fleeing forced conscription into the Tsar's army, where Jews faced long service and open discrimination. Hoda later reconnected with her brothers, and for many years, Louis sent a money order for U.S.$50—welcome support and a reminder of family.

Hoda stood about 5 feet, 3 inches tall and was appealingly *zaftig*, plump. She had a full figure, long legs and thick dark brown hair that she wore in a low bun. Her face was pretty, with a small nose, high cheekbones, olive complexion and soft dark eyes that missed nothing. Hoda was a powerhouse. What she lacked in height, she made up for in presence. She had little time for idle gossip and as a result she tended to favour male company over female.

The story of Hoda's *shidduch* (arranged marriage) aptly sums up my indomitable grandmother. When Rav Yosef Schuster arrived from Eishyshok to meet his intended, he took one look at his future bride and happily consented to the match. Hoda, on the other hand, had some conditions before agreeing to the marriage. Though traditionally observant, she was also very modern. In spite of not having a formal secular education, Hoda was naturally intelligent and a very progressive thinker, a feminist well ahead of her time. My twenty-three-year-old grandmother told her thirty-two-year-old suitor that she would adhere to the codes of modest dress for women required by Jewish law, but she would do so her way. She would not, for example, wrap up all her hair in a *tichel*, a headscarf, so none of it showed. Rather, she would cover her locks with a conservative loose black shawl for every day and with a white one for synagogue. More importantly, contrary to a custom still practiced today in ultra-Orthodox communities whereby the wife is the breadwinner so her husband can pursue religious studies, Hoda made it clear that Rav Yosef needed to earn a living.

She was not going to marry a man whose life goal and profession was to *kvetchen dem benkel* (wear down the little bench), a great Yiddish idiom for someone glued to his bottom studying (religious texts) all day, instead of working or engaging in more worldly affairs. Rav Yosef had his *semicha*, rabbinical ordination—that was enough religious knowledge for Hoda. She was ready and willing to do her part to help but insisted Rav Yosef go into business. He was obviously a very astute man who recognized Hoda was a very special woman. He agreed to her conditions and did exactly what she asked. My grandparents were married on April 2, 1904, in Pumpyan, and true to his promise Rav Yosef went into business. I believe his family had a bakery, so he chose the flour business, doing very well in the early years. But the business went bankrupt at the end of World War I, a casualty of the conflict and of Rav Yosef's untimely death in 1918, of typhus.

Hoda was now a young widow with seven children to raise. Basia, age eleven at the time, was the eldest. (A firstborn child was stillborn.) Rivke, age one, was the youngest. Between them were Chaya Sarah, David, Chaim, Nechama, and Moshe (Meyshele). It was a sore point with Hoda her entire life that none of Rav Yosef's sisters, already settled in the United States, offered to lighten her load by taking one or more of her children to live with them in America.

Meyshele was apparently very gifted. At age four he was able to read an entire *blatt* (a single page, front and back) of Gemara, a foundational commentary on Jewish laws and teachings. I imagine he would have done great things with a mind like his. Unfortunately, he died within a very short period of my grandfather's death, possibly also from typhus. He was only five years old. These tragedies left Hoda feeling abandoned by God. Reb Zundel Hutner, Eishyshok's rabbi, sent a messenger telling her not to despair. Hoda apparently told him that if God could forsake her when she most needed Him, then Reb Zundel himself should have been God's earthly agent, not a messenger. Reb Zundel responded with another message, telling her that he understood her plight. Hoda was even less impressed. But she did come away with a valuable life lesson. She determined from then on to never go through an intermediary. From that day forward my grandmother was her own spokeswoman. She interacted directly with people and never used a go-between to negotiate for her.

Following the deaths of her husband and son, there was really no choice for Hoda. A survivor through and through, she understood that she needed a new venture that would provide for herself and her young family. Hoda had a good knowledge of fabrics and an excellent head for business, so she chose the textile business. There were many women shopkeepers in Eishyshok, but I believe only one other woman was in the textile business at the same time as my grandmother in the early 1930s.

Rad kromen, Eishyshok, late 1920s.
PERMISSION FOR USE GRANTED BY: YAFFA ELIACH SHTETL COLLECTION

The best stores in town were located in the *rad kromen*—a strip of small shops, called *kremlach*, set side by side in the centre of Eishyshok's market square. The most profitable trade took place here. The number of stores, their locations and their leases were governed by law through the *kahal*, the municipal governing authority.

The leases were hereditary, handed down within families from generation to generation, making it virtually impossible for a newcomer to gain a foothold in a prime retail location on the market square. What galled Hoda even more was that the most successful textile shop owner in town, Yosel Weidenberg, led the other merchants in blocking her for a time from acquiring one of these coveted leases. I believe Hoda appealed to the kahal and lost, and I remember that battle left a bitter taste in her mouth.

At some point, Hoda did open a store. Despite it being outside the main square, the store flourished. By 1939, we were comfortably off. Hoda was very generous about extending credit to her customers. When we left Eishyshok there were dozens of small credit slips called *vekhslakh* from customers who would later survive the war. My bobe never collected on those debts from any of those survivors.

The success of Hoda's business was due in no small part to the sacrifice of my mother's childhood. Hoda understood that she could not run a store on her own. The only way she could hope to make the shop profitable was with an able and trustworthy right hand. As the eldest child, that person was Basia. She had to quit school to work full-time. This was a huge blow for her, having to abandon her studies so young.

Basia took the mantle of responsibility thrust upon her, doing whatever needed to be done to make the business a success. She was the salesperson, cashier and bookkeeper. Hoda was the buyer. After Basia married Moshe, he handled the accounting. And Rivke would help out during very busy times.

I remember as a little girl of age four that the store seemed rather shabby and dark. But one particular feature had great appeal. In the winter, I would go straight to it—a large cast iron pot with burning coals below and a wire mesh cover across the top. My mother and grandmother wore fingerless gloves and in cold weather they would place their hands above the pot to warm them. It was far easier for them to cut fabric with warm hands than cold ones, so the coals were always stoked to make sure there was adequate heat to keep the store's temperature at a comfortable level.

Sometime around 1936 or 1937 the rad kromen burned down and was rebuilt. It was not the first time, as fires were a not infrequent occurrence in Eishyshok. The rad kromen was always rebuilt in the same location, as dictated by law. The latest one boasted row shops that were much nicer than the old ones. More importantly, Bobe managed to secure a lease on one of these shops. The new premises were far more modern and, in my eyes, exceptionally fine.

Our new store boasted glass from top to bottom and had beautiful lighting. Gone was the glove-warming pot. In its place was a proper heating system. The store's wares were now beautifully displayed on shelves worthy of a grand retailer in a larger city. Hoda had a wonderful eye for colour and texture, and the store was chock full of beautiful bolts of cloth and trimmings. I loved going around the shelves and touching every piece of fabric and inspecting the trimming. The fabrics were exquisite, with exotic French names that I revelled in learning to pronounce: *peau de soie, georgette, marquisette, mousseline.*

Those early days roaming the shelves of my bobe's store gave me a lifelong love for textiles. Like the visual memories of my aunt Rachil in Vilna, I have equally strong memories of my grandmother putting together her daughter's wedding trousseau. Rivke chose a magnificent mousseline, a fine French muslin, with a mix of blue, green, coral and gold. It was made into a gorgeous dressing gown, with a lovely Turkish design and a beautiful satin lining in a complementary shade of blue. The impression of this loungewear was deep and lasting. I even had something made for myself when I was older that was a derivative of that design.

Hoda used to go on buying trips, journeying long distances to find the best fabrics for the store. She often travelled to Lvov in western Ukraine, about six hundred kilometres south of Eishyshok, and to Krakow, Poland, a further hundred kilometres west. She always came home from these trips with gifts for me and her other granddaughter, Shayna Rivke Kamjonski, the daughter of my aunt Chaya Sarah. The Kamjonski family lived in a town called Ostryn, about 100 kilometres southeast of Eishyshok, near the Belorussian-Polish border. My aunt, her husband, Yankel, Shayna Rivke and her younger brother, Chaim Yosef, often visited and joined us for the holidays. Chaya Sarah and my mother bore a strong resemblance to one another. Yankel had actually wanted to marry Basia, but she felt too much responsibility for her mother, so my mother made the successful match for her sister instead of for herself, and Chaya Sarah married Yankel.

Shayna Rivke was born with a heart defect and her lips always had a faint blue tinge. When she came to visit she would climb onto Bobe's lap, and like a little bull with a red flag raised before its eyes, I would charge, scrambling up beside Shayna Rivke to send her a clear message that Bobe's lap was my domain. Bobe, of course, thought we were both equally precious. And somehow, like magic, the lap of my little grandmother would grow to accommodate both my cousin and me.

After one of her trips to Krakow, Bobe returned with two little pillbox hats, one blue, the other red. I can still picture them, with their white felt diamond cut-outs and long white tassels. The hats were beautiful and reminded me of *hamentashen*, the tri-cornered cookies eaten on the mid-winter holiday of Purim and named for Haman, the villain in the Purim story. The cookie's shape is said to symbolize his three-cornered hat (or his ears). Shayna Rivke had blond hair and very blue eyes so she got the blue hat. Another time Bobe came home with a white rabbit coat, with matching hat, mittens and a little muff on a cord, for each of us. I remember my cousin and I parading around like princesses in those beautiful coats and accessories.

When I think back to my childhood in Eishyshok until age six, I remember them as the happiest of my early life. However, what I am unable to do is summon a picture in my mind of the overall town. I think it is because I never went anywhere on my own; I was too young.

One of the earliest memories I have, from around age three or four, was of going with my mother to the dressmaker to have new clothes made for me for the High Holy Days—Rosh Hashanah (Jewish New Year) and Yom Kippur (Day of Atonement)—the most important holidays of the Jewish calendar. All our clothes were made by seamstresses, with fabric from our store. My mother usually dressed me in navy blue and white, sometimes with red accents. My hair was very long and my mother was constantly playing with it and devising new hair styles. I often wore it parted in the centre, with two French braids on either side of my crown feeding into two long braids that hung down to my waist and were tied with shantung ribbons to match the accent colour on my outfit. All my dresses were short, with a soft A-line silhouette. I remember one especially beautiful navy dress made from a very fine wool, with wide-pinched pleats from a yoked bodice, a white silk baby collar and narrow white manchettes.

My best friend was Ritka Schwarz. We were like sisters. Our parents even dressed us alike. Ritka's family were well-to-do merchants. I loved going to her place because she had huge dolls and a large dollhouse the size of a room. We would go inside it and play house.

My family's house was more modest than Ritka's, but very comfortable and cheery. We lived in a fourplex. Our home had a salon and dining room, with lovely long lace curtains, called *gardine*, hanging in the windows of each room. The dining room had a large rectangular oak table and chairs, and a breakfront where we kept all our dishes. The table was the centre of the space. It was where our family ate, where we hosted guests and where Papa worked. It was also where Papa kept a large abacus with feet. He also had a smaller abacus and a child-sized one for me. From my vantage as a little girl, the large abacus seemed gigantic. Papa would move it from the table as needed when we ate or when he played chess.

In addition to the salon and dining room, we had three bedrooms. One was for Bobe Hoda, one was for Rivke, and the third bedroom was Mama and Papa's. I slept in the same room as my parents, on a pretty little nickel and white enamel youth bed. If we had overnight visitors Rivke shared her mother's bedroom.

On one of the dining room walls in our home hung a photo of my grandfather, Rav Yosef Schuster, and a photo of the Vilna *Gaon*, the great eighteenth-century Talmudist. I remember the great rabbi's photo looked grey and that he wore a hat, as opposed to my grandfather, who wore a *kippah*, a Jewish skullcap. I was very impressed by the Vilna Gaon's hat.

The vestibule of our fourplex had four doors leading to each of its four units. There was one unit along each side of the building, and two units at the rear. On the extreme left as you entered lived our *chazzan*, our cantor, Moshe Tobolski, his pretty wife, Rivke, and their two beautiful daughters, Shayndele and Zinale.

Shayndele was two years older than me and Zinale a year younger. We were a tight little threesome, always playing games and having fun, regularly going in and out of each other's apartments. Our parents were also good friends and often visited each other.

Moshe Tobolski had a magnificent voice, a lyric tenor. Young and popular, he was also very handsome, especially in his formal cantorial

Main synagogue, Eishyshok, c. 1940.

PERMISSION FOR USE GRANTED BY: YAFFA ELIACH SHTETL COLLECTION

garb of long black silk coat and his black *keppel*, a stiff cantorial cap favoured by European cantors. The entire shtetl revered our chazzan. He sang with such passion and emotion I think the angels cried when they heard him. He was also an excellent musician and led the choir at our *shul*, the synagogue.

I yearned to be in his choir. I loved music and started singing around age four. Notwithstanding my age, I did not stand a chance of realizing my dream as mixed gender chorale groups are not part of Orthodox tradition. That impediment may have kept me from officially being part of the choir, but it did not stop the chazzan from teaching me all the repertoire. I would sit on his lap and we would practise all the songs together, or I would sit on Papa's lap pretending I was a choir member. Papa and I were familiar fixtures at the chazzan's home when he rehearsed for the High Holy Days and Shabbat, the Jewish Sabbath.

I was enchanted watching the chazzan lead his singers. I really liked his *kamerton*, a two-pronged tuning fork. It was such a funny little instrument. When hit on the table it vibrated, producing its one note, an A, and everyone would start singing scales. I did not do the

Chazzan Tobolski's Final Prayer

On the eve of Rosh Hashanah 1941, Eishyshok's Jews were rounded up and locked in the synagogue and two schools. After three days, they were herded to the horse market, led by Rabbi Szyman Rozowski, holding a Torah scroll, and by Chazzan Tobolski, who recited the *Viddui*—the traditional deathbed confessional prayer—with everyone.

Over the next two days, the Jews were taken in groups of 250—first the men and then the women and children—to the old Jewish cemetery. They were ordered to undress and stand at the edge of large open ditches, where they were shot to death by Lithuanian police. Babies were bashed to death against headstones or tossed into the air for sharpshooting practice led by the chief of police, Ostrauskas, before their tiny lifeless or quivering bodies were thrown into the killing pits to join their parents. Everyone was murdered, including Chazzan Tobolski, Rivke, Shayndele and Zinale, and Eishyshok's rabbi, and Rabbi Szyman Rozowski, the final victim of the massacre. He was shot after being forced to witness the murder of his entire flock.

scales with everyone. I sat there bewildered during the warm-up. Even so, I still felt that I was a full-fledged member of the group. Pretty soon I learned all the melodies and lyrics by heart, and with everyone's full encouragement I sang along with the members of the choir when they came to practice. My sweet child's soprano imitated every nuance of the chazzan, and Papa *shepped naches*, beamed with pride. I can still see the smiles he and Chazzan Tobolski exchanged with one another and with the men from the choir. I sometimes flash back to this time when I hear the beautiful voice of the chazzan in my shul, especially when he sings the *Unetanah Tokef* prayer on Yom Kippur eve, ushering in the beginning of this holy day of atonement and fasting.

I made my singing debut at age four at a recital with a group of young performers. I was the youngest. My mother was very concerned that I should look beautiful and I remember she untied my braids so my hair flowed in long beautiful waves. It was parted on one side and clipped on the other with a large white shantung bow. I did not have an appropriate dress to wear for the concert, so my mother borrowed one from Zinale. She and her sister were very excited about me wearing Zinale's dress for my debut. It was champagne coloured, frilly, full-skirted and very short. I remember not liking that I had to wear slightly longer panties so I would not get cold. The other disappointment was my shoes. I wanted to wear the popular rounded toe, one-strap Mary Janes so I would be fashionable like the other girls. Shaynele and Zinale got to wear them. But my mother insisted I wear spats so my ankles would be supported.

I sang a little song in Hebrew called "Ha Tzipor," about a small bird that comes to rest on the windowsill of a child's home and flies away when the child tries to reach for it. This makes the child very sad. In addition to learning the song, I also learned accompanying hand gestures to convey the child's sorrow. Clearly I succeeded beyond all measure, as my family and our friends threw large chocolates onto the stage when I was done. I am sure this tribute was inspired by Aunt Rivke, who knew I had a sweet tooth. I had practised in front of a mirror how to curtsy in my dress, and after I finished my performance I flaunted my new skill, gracefully curtsying multiple times. Then, most definitely much less gracefully, I bent down to scoop up the chocolates before returning to sit with my most adoring fans—my family and the Tobolskis. I relished everyone's praise, especially my aunt's. She told me that I sang like an angel.

One of the other two units in our building was occupied by a lovely family with two young children. The father, Sioma, was a painter and very gentle, like my father. A small man with a hunched back, he had a kind face and deeply set, inquiring eyes. Sioma and his wife occasionally invited me over to their home for *wieczerza*, a light supper. Our custom, like most of Europe, was to have a heavier main meal at midday. Offices would close between two o'clock and four o'clock, and employees would go home to dine with their families. I remember Sioma's wife served fine handmade egg noodles called *lokshen*, with milk. This was a real treat for me since Hoda did not like slippery foods like lokshen and did not make them. The remaining residents of our building were a couple, Reb Alter and his wife, Chaya. I had little contact with them, but Reb Alter's death left an indelible impression on me.

I was about age four or five. In shtetls like ours, when someone passed away, the *tahara*, the ritual purification of the body for burial, was performed in the home of the deceased by the *chevra kadisha*, the Jewish burial society. Clutching Papa's hand, I entered Reb Alter's apartment after the chevra kadisha were finished preparing his body. Alter was lying on the floor in his *tachrichim*, traditional white linen burial shrouds, with a stone on each of his closed eyes. Tall, lit candles in candlesticks surrounded his body, creating a very tranquil aura.

Papa told me Alter's *neshama*, his soul, was now in Olam Haba, the next world, and that only his body remained in this world. He put a finger over his lips and I understood Papa could not speak with me further in that moment out of respect for Alter's neshama. The men of the chevra kadisha wrapped Alter's body up in a sheet and began saying special prayers. After the prayers were over, I noticed a man in the corner with his lips still moving. "Why is that man still praying when everyone stopped?" I asked Papa. "That man is different from the others," he explained. "He is saying special psalms called *tehillim* to help guide Alter's soul to Olam Haba. He will stay with Alter until they take him to be buried, which will be soon."

It is not every day a little girl sees a dead body at her neighbour's home. I still had a lot of questions for my father. "Why did they put those stones on Alter's closed eyes?" I asked Papa. He told me the clay shards are called *sharvens*, and that the little pieces of earthenware were placed as a symbol of returning to the dust of the earth. "What about food?" I wondered aloud. "The dead do not need food," Papa answered. I was increasingly bewildered. Every answer begat a follow-up question. "Why were Alter's feet facing the entryway to the apartment?" I wanted to know. "It means his soul is ready to exit this world. It means he is ready to say good-bye to everyone," said Papa. "To me, too?" I asked. "Definitely," said Papa. "Because he loved you, too."

I watched as several of the men moved Alter's wrapped body onto some wooden planks. There was no casket. The men lifted the planks and carried Alter out of the apartment and put him into the back of a buggy. He was then taken to the cemetery for burial. I did not go to the interment. The sheet I saw earlier on the floor of his home was no longer in the apartment when I went back inside our building. After the funeral, each time I passed by Alter's door I still had visions of him lying on that floor.

My life mostly revolved around the Tobolskis' house, my friend Ritka's house, my house and the store. With Mama and Bobe occupied with the shop, I spent a lot of time with Papa and Aunt Rivke. My aunt was very attractive. She was built like her sisters, tall and long-legged, but that is where the resemblance ended. Rivke had large blue eyes, dark eyelashes and fair skin. She had perfect eyebrows, a milky complexion, full lips and beautiful wavy medium blond hair that hung down to her waist. I was told that she and her brother David looked a lot alike. Rivke loved plants and had a green thumb. When it rained, she would schlep our heavy potted ficus plants outside to be nourished by the rainfall. The plants would be left out until evening and taken back inside after they had received a good soaking. Rivke explained to me that aside from nourishing our houseplants the rainwater was especially good for washing one's hair, which she did. Often. The fresh rainwater must have worked, because her hair was like shining silk. Just gorgeous.

Aunt Rivke Schuster, Berlin, 1946.
COURTESY OF EVELYN KAHN

Rivke was far less serious in nature than Basia. As the youngest in the family, she enjoyed the luxury of bearing fewer of the heavy responsibilities. She loved beautiful clothes and had a good eye for colour and quality. Aunt Rivke loved to give me kisses and to pamper and spoil me. She took me for my first manicure around the age of

Rivke and Noach's tenaim (betrothal), Eishyshok, 1938.
Seated (l-r): Shayndele and Zinale Tobolski (far left), Rivke and Noach (centre), Yisroel Bielski, Motl Bielski, and unknown man (front)
Standing (l-r): Rivka Tobolski (far left), Evelyn, Bobe Hoda, Chaim Schuster, Basia and Moshe Landsman, Sioma's widow, unknown women (far right)
COURTESY OF EVELYN KAHN

four. I chose a warm shade of orange lacquer for my nails—I thought they looked yummy. My aunt had a wonderful sense of humour, with a ready laugh so hearty it often brought tears to her eyes.

Rivke was engaged when she was about age eighteen to a man named Noach. In the days leading up to their engagement party, there was great hustle and bustle in our home. Bobe, Mama and Aunt Rivke prepared all manner of special gastronomic delights, including *ptcha*, jellied calf's feet topped with sliced egg. I loved the taste of ptcha but it was challenging to eat, as it was slippery and hard to spear with my fork. The rich torte my aunt made was far easier to enjoy—and more delicious. I can still taste its rich chocolate buttercream between layers of thin crunchy wafers, and the chocolate ganache icing—a chocoholic's dream.

One of my lasting memories from the betrothal party was the breaking of a plate by Hoda with Noach's mother. This ritual marked the completion of the *tenaim*, the terms of the betrothal. As it turned out, the plate was not the only thing that ended up broken. Shortly thereafter, so was the engagement. I do not know if Rivke was heartbroken. But I certainly was not. I was delighted. As far as I was concerned, Noach's loss was my gain. I loved being with Aunt Rivke and I had not been all that keen on sharing her.

Rivke handled the bulk of the household cleaning and daily upkeep. My aunt took a lot of pride in our apartment. She kept it immaculate and orderly. The floors in our home were coarsely finished wood planks and my aunt made sure they were always spotless. She would work on them until they sparkled.

The heart of our house was the kitchen. It had counters of dark wood and a large hearth with a wood-burning ceramic oven, which doubled as our home heating system. In one part of the kitchen was a *katukh*, a dark little hollow space underneath the counter where we kept our chickens until we took them to be slaughtered by the *shochet*, the ritual slaughterer. The katukh was covered by a little gingham curtain. The chickens used to make a lot of noise and I was afraid

Illustration based on Evelyn's recollection of the katukh in her family home in Eishyshok.

of the katukh, especially after one of the chickens got out and ran around the kitchen in an effort to escape.

On the eve of Yom Kippur my father performed a once-a-year ritual called *kaparot* with one of those chickens. He reached into the katukh , grabbed a rooster by the feet and carefully passed it over his head three times while reciting a special prayer asking the Almighty for forgiveness. My father then donated the fowl to the butcher to be humanely slaughtered and given to a poor person for a pre-fast meal. I can still hear the mad clucking of that rooster and see the wild flapping of his wings.

As in most shtetls in Eastern Europe, the rhythm of life in Eishyshok was modulated by the Jewish calendar. The apex of the week was Shabbat, the holiest and most special day. Shabbat preparations began in earnest on Thursday, when Bobe Hoda and Rivke made the rounds in the shtetl's market square, visiting the different vendors and stocking up on provisions, carefully selecting the best fresh produce, poultry and meat. They would return home loaded with groceries and begin advance preparations for Shabbat. Delicious aromas filled every room of the house.

We had to make sure everything was cooked and ready before sunset on Friday night since we were forbidden by Jewish law to do any work on the Shabbat. Like most Jewish families in Eishyshok, we engaged a gentile, called a *sabbotnik*, to do certain chores on Shabbat that we were prohibited from doing ourselves, for example lighting a fire. Our sabbotnik, a woman, came just before Shabbat began on Friday evening to light the wood under the oven. In the cold months she also came on Saturday. Hoda did most of the cooking; Rivke, the baking. My aunt was a wonderful baker.

I was encouraged to observe and was happy to do so. It was like watching a cooking show. My bobe worked quickly and efficiently. She was an intuitive cook, with a culinary style that seemed mysterious and a bit whimsical to me. I can still hear my grandmother, with laughter in her voice, explaining to me her "recipe" for everything. "Nem a bissel fun dem, oon a bissel fun yenem. Oon ala mol farzuk tsu zighn geshmack (Take a little from this, and a little from that. And keep tasting until it's delicious)," she said. Then, passing me her spoon, she'd add "Chavale, farzukh (taste)," and I rendered

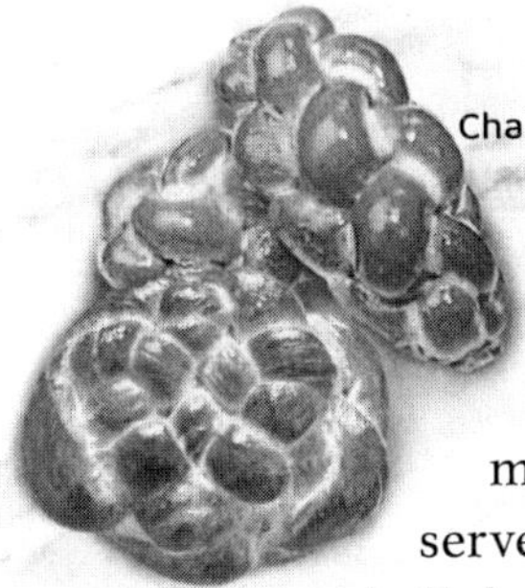
Challah

my opinion. "Geshmack, Bobe (Delicious, grandmother)," I declared.

Shabbat meal preparations began with making *challah*, the traditional braided bread served on Sabbath and festivals. Bobe Hoda's challahs were most beautiful. I especially liked to watch as she prepared the yeast for the dough. I took great delight as its foamy head rose higher and higher in the *shisel*, a white and blue enamel bowl, before sometimes overflowing onto the counter and then joining the flour that had already sprinkled in snowy drifts onto the kitchen floor.

My grandmother kneaded the dough on the counter, and when she was satisfied with the texture she placed the dough in a bowl, covered it with a towel and set it aside to rise. Once the dough had risen enough, Hoda punched it down and sectioned it into long doughy ropes that she then braided together to form beautiful challah loaves. The loaves were left to rise again, and when my bobe was satisfied they were ready she placed them into the oven to bake. I can still smell the sweet aroma of those baking challahs. For the High Holy Days my grandmother made beautiful round challahs with exquisite designs.

Next came the *gefilte*, or stuffed fish. Bobe Hoda made authentically Litvisher (Lithuanian-style) gefilte fish. Rich, moist and savoury—the best. It was made with a mixture of local lake fish, usually a nice meaty carp, and another equally fatty white fish that would not dry out during the long cooking process. I loved, with equal parts awe and apprehension, to watch her prepare it.

My grandmother bought whole fish at the market and brought them home alive in a container of water. She removed each fish from the water and placed it on a wooden board on the counter, holding fast to make sure it did not flop away. I remember the carp was huge. I stood at Bobe's side as she hit the fish on the head with her wooden mallet. Sometimes the fish trembled a bit afterwards and that scared me. I really did not like to see the fish tremble, and I definitely did not like the dead fish eyes that stared back at me when it was finally still—all of which may explain why as a little girl I did not actually eat my bobe's gefilte fish.

Each fish was cleaned and filleted, except the carp, which Hoda cut into slices about an inch thick. She scooped out the centre of each slice, leaving them clean and hollowed out. Next, she took the scooped-out flesh and minced it together with the other fish and combined them with onions she had sautéed in oil until they were a rich dark brown. She then added salt, pepper, raw eggs, a little *matzoh* meal (finely ground unleavened bread) and some sugar, tasting and adjusting the flavour as she added ingredients. When the flavour of the mixture was just right, Hoda carefully stuffed some mixture inside the empty centres of the hollowed-out slices. The stuffed slices were then placed into a pot filled with fish stock she had prepared earlier with the cleaned bones and heads of the fish, onions, carrots and seasoning, and the pot was covered to let the fish poach for a few hours. The gefilte fish slices were served at room temperature, with horseradish and a slice of carrot garnish.

Years later Basia dropped the whole process of stuffing the fish into the hollowed-out slices and adopted a more "modern" approach, using prepared fish from the market and making oval-shaped gefilte fish balls without any skin. By that time, I was able to help. And it was always easy to tell which fish balls were mine, as my small hands formed the smallest balls. At some point my mother also added pike and whitefish to the carp, which is the mixture I still like to use. It was not until I began making gefilte fish on my own that I learned to love this traditional dish and appreciate how much work goes into preparing it.

No Shabbat meal was complete without Hoda's chicken soup and *kreplach*, little dumplings of very fine dough stuffed with ground beef. At Pesach (Passover), fluffy round *kneydlakh* (matzoh balls) replaced the kreplach.

Our main course was either chicken, duck or beef, with a side of *tzimmes*, a sweet side dish of stewed carrots, prunes and roast potatoes. Fresh vegetables were scarce, so they were rare. The only ones I remember were cucumber, radish, tomato and green onion, which appeared in the summer months. For dessert we had a compote of dried apples, pears and prunes stewed with lemon and sugar. In the summer months we had fresh strawberries, blueberries and raspberries with sugar. We also had honey cake and light, almost weightless cookies called *kichelach*. Tea with lemon was served Russian style, piping hot in

Kichelach

Bobe Hode's podstakan

a glass fit into a *podstakan*, a metal holder with a handle.

It was the custom for Bobe Hoda before sundown on Friday to prepare our *cholent*, the hearty, slow-cooked stew that we ate at our midday meal on Saturday. My grandmother cooked it in a large cast-iron pot. Her cholent included chunks of meat (the fattier the better), sautéed onions, potatoes, a smattering of large lima beans, stuffed beef intestine called *kishke* and some salt and pepper. Sometimes she mixed flour, eggs, shmaltz, a little onion, salt and garlic to make a small *kugele*, a little baked pudding that she would place on top of the cholent to cook. The pot was filled with enough water to cover the meat and vegetables to ensure a moist stew. The lid was secured and Rivke took our cholent to the town baker, where it joined dozens of other cholents to cook overnight on a low heat in his oven. Bobe used to tie a small ribbon around the handle of our cholent pot so we could easily identify ours from all the others at the baker. But sometimes ribbons would fall off or someone would grab the wrong pot, and families ended up enjoying someone else's cholent. I do not recall if this ever happened to us. But if it did, some family got very lucky if they got my bobe's. After synagogue on Saturday, Papa, Rivke and I would retrieve our pot and bring it home for a hearty lunch.

My own Shabbat preparations consisted of being washed and bathed before Shabbat candle lighting. While these tasks seem simple enough, they were still somewhat labour intensive. We had no indoor plumbing and hence no running water. (The grown-ups did their business in the outhouse at the back of the building. I did mine inside our home, in a little white enamel potty.) The water we used in our home was drawn at the communal well and carried into our house by hired water carriers. No mean feat. They carried two pails at a time strung on a pole that was borne across their shoulders and then emptied into a large copper pot placed on the stove. Once the water was heated in the pot it was poured into a copper bathing tub, and in I went. My body was scrubbed, my hair washed, and I came out rosy and fresh, ready to dress in my Shabbat finery to greet the "Shabbat Queen," the metaphorical royal presence who encapsulates the reverence and love for the Shabbat, and brings peace, rest and spiritual renewal.

As sundown approached on Friday, a calm descended on our home. I would get very excited when just before sunset the *shamas* (sexton) called "In shul arein (It's time to be in shul)!" Papa would leave for synagogue. While he was at prayers, Bobe, her hair covered in a white lace shawl, followed by Mama and then Rivke, would usher in Shabbat at home by *benching licht*, blessing the Shabbat candles in our beautiful shining silver candlesticks. Aunt Rivke and I did not light Shabbat candles, as it was not our custom for single women to do so. Neither was it our custom for the women to go to shul on Friday nights. Just Papa went.

When my father returned home from synagogue we took our seats at the Shabbat table, which was covered with a fine white tablecloth and set resplendently with our finest dishes, stemware and sparkling cutlery. The warm golden challahs were placed on their tray and covered with an embroidered cover. Bathed in the soft glow of the Shabbat lights, Papa filled his cup with wine and led us in *kiddush*, the ritual blessing over the wine. From the time I was very young, I always felt very close to God. But right after Papa finished the blessing over the wine I remember the special moment of feeling Hashem, the Divine presence of God, with all of us. After we finished eating, we said the *birkat hamazon*, grace after the meals.

Saturday morning, my father and I went to shul. The rest of the family followed later. Our wooden synagogue building had two storeys, with separate seating for men and women according to Orthodox tradition. The men's section was on the main floor, with the *aron kodesh* (holy ark), containing the Torah scrolls, and the *bimah*, the raised platform from where the Torah was read and services were led. The women's section was on a second-floor balcony overlooking the men's section, where we could watch and hear the services below.

I loved going to shul on Shabbat morning with my father to hear Chazzan Tobolski chant the prayers. My mother would send me off with a small handkerchief tied closed at the corners that she filled with treats of cookies and candies. When I got to shul, I would carefully untie the knot and treat myself to one of my goodies while the adults prayed. I was not a good eater as a child, so seeing me eat my Shabbat treats gave my mother great delight.

After lunch on Shabbat afternoon people visited and took tea served from our large brass samovar. The urn always seemed to have more than enough water for us and all our Shabbat guests. It was customary after all that eating to go for a leisurely stroll, *shpatziren*. Going shpatziren on Saturday afternoon was not only good for digestion, it was also a great way for people to socialize and admire each other's Shabbat outfits.

Shabbat was active, but nothing compared to Pesach (Passover). How ambitious Rivke became before the holiday, channelling the holiday's theme of rebirth to our home! Everything had to be spick and span, without a grain of *chametz* (leavened food) left in the house.

Around mid- to late March, in a sure sign that Pesach was on the way, communal matzoh baking hives would sprout up and produce huge batches of handmade matzohs. The hives were called *podryat*, Russian for "continuous communal effort." It is an apt term for the coordinated, assembly-line nature of the matzoh baking process, which had to be completed in eighteen minutes from the time the flour had contact with the water until the well-kneaded dough was formed into flat round discs, perforated and put into the large ovens to bake. I liked to watch the big round matzohs come out of the oven. Even the burnt ones were pretty. The matzohs had to be handled very carefully so they would not break. When Pesach came, my father, Rivke and I would go to the podryat to collect our matzohs. We would place our precious and very fragile cargo carefully into pillow cases and walk home, I with my small pillow case and Papa and Rivke with two large ones apiece across each of their shoulders. Although I enjoyed watching the process of producing matzoh, I hated the taste of it. I still do.

Despite my aversion to the holiday's key food, I have cherished memories of Pesach—especially *seder* (Hebrew for "order"). The seder is an experiential meal held on the eve of the first night of the holiday (first and second nights outside Israel), designed to commemorate the Exodus—the Jewish journey from slavery in Egypt to freedom—using symbolic foods, storytelling, songs, rituals and prayers. The choreography of the evening is set out in a special book called a Haggadah. Much of the ceremony takes place before the meal itself, and it can be several hours before dinner is finally served.

On seder night, Papa was the leader and sat at the head of the table propped up with large feather pillows at his back to symbolize freedom, the core theme of the Passover story. Free people have the luxury of

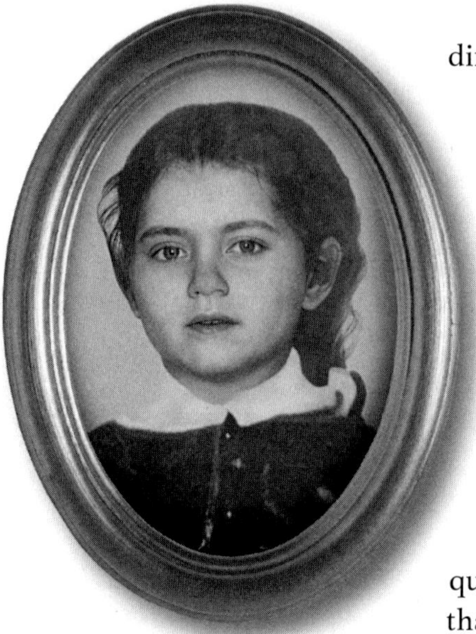

Evelyn, age six, Eishyshok, 1939. (The only photo the author has of herself as a child.)
COURTESY OF EVELYN KAHN

dining leisurely, in contrast to slaves, who must eat in haste. I sat next to my father and Mama next to me.

I especially loved the years when our Kamjonski cousins joined us for Pesach. Uncle Yankel, Aunt Chaya Sarah and my cousins, Shayna Rivke and Chaim Yosef, would sit across the table from me. I envied Chaim Yosef at Pesach because he was the youngest, which meant he got to sing the four *kashehs*, the traditional four questions of "Ma Nishtanah," the song that queries "Why is this night different from all other nights?" I longed to sing the song. But the tradition was that the youngest person at the table sings it.

Seders are deeply child-centred, with rituals designed to spark curiosity and questions meant to ensure the story of the Jewish people is passed from generation to generation. Midway through the pre-dinner part of the seder, Papa would break a piece of matzoh and hide half of it. This hidden half was the *afikomen* (from the Greek word *epikomon*, meaning "dessert"). The meal was not officially over and the remainder of the seder could not continue until Papa broke up the afikomen and distributed a small piece to everyone. But first I had to find it—and collect my reward.

Hunting for the afikomen was my favourite part of the seder. I could not wait to begin my search. I had to walk around the table to get to the salon, where I carefully made my way around the room. When I was very young, the grown-ups helped guide me with little winks and nods, directing me away from the curtains or towards the pillows on the sofa. I was ecstatic when I located the treasure. "I found it. I found it!" I would shout with glee and return it to Papa for my reward: one zloty! I kept my prize safely under my pillow until I spent it—on chocolate. When I was completely stumped, I remember Papa made the afikomen magically appear—as did my złoty.

Seders are lengthy ordeals. And ours were no different. By the time we ate dinner and I had searched for the afikomen, I inevitably fell asleep at the table and had to be carried to bed. I tried so hard to keep my eyes open long enough to see the prophet Eliyahu, the symbol of hope and future redemption of the Jewish people. He was said to "visit" every seder, like a Jewish Santa Claus, but without the presents.

"Oh, Papa, I missed Eilyahu," I would tell my father when I awoke the morning after seder.

"Yes, you nearly made it. You barely missed him," my father would respond encouragingly, hiding a smile.

And then I promised Papa that the following year I would stay up and catch the prophet.

I definitely enjoyed the orderly anticipation leading up to Pesach, but I confess that the end of the holiday held much more appeal for me. When Pesach was just over and the aromas from the Jewish bakeries began to permeate the town, my mouth would water as I smelled the scent of cookies, especially the kichelach. My father, who could never deny me anything, took me to the bakery the minute it was open so I could indulge my sweet tooth. It felt very stealthy. Papa and I would descend the stairs to the bakery where the bakers were busy packing orders. I would emerge with a sweet pastry, which I wasted no time in devouring, eliciting a broad smile on Papa's face. After having to eat matzoh for a whole week I welcomed the treat with delight and to this day cannot wait until I am liberated from the restrictions of Pesach.

We used to bring our gentile neighbours matzoh and wine at Pesach. But I do not recall them ever inviting us for Easter. (Maybe they liked matzoh as much as I?) I do recall being invited in to see their beautiful Christmas tree when we visited in December. I remember the lovely trimmings and the angel at the top. I also recall the many wooden crosses displayed on every wall in their home, which I found slightly disturbing. I never knew why the crosses bothered me; they just gave me a sense of foreboding. I remember being offered candy and lots of very pretty decorated cookies with red sprinkles and multi-coloured frosting, very different from my grandmother's baking. I looked at Papa to check if it was okay to take them home with me. He taught me to be gracious and instructed me to accept the gift and to say thank you. But I never ate these homemade treats, as they were not kosher. Papa disposed of them when I got home.

From time to time, we took in boarders. One of these was Motl (Mordechai) Bielski, who commuted between Eishyshok and Zhetel, where he lived with his family. Motl reminded me very much of Papa, both in demeanor and looks. He had the same gentle nature as Papa and the same happy face, bright eyes and dark hair. Even their builds were similar. Motl just had smaller shoulders. He taught at the Hebrew school I could see from the window of our dining room. I used to stand by that window and look longingly out at the children playing in the schoolyard, yearning for the day I could join them. Thanks to Motl, I got my wish.

Being an only child, I was a bit precocious, which did not escape the man's notice. He spoke with the school principal, Moshe Yaakov Botwinik, and I was admitted to kindergarten a year early. I remember how excited I was at the prospect of going to school. I even recall one of my first projects: a top hat with shiny black and white and red paper. Motl's wife, Malka, and their sons, Yosef and Yisroel, sometimes visited him. Yosef was my age and Yisroel around four years younger. I particularly liked Yosef and remember hiding with him under the dining table while the adults had tea, chastely playing doctor with him. Our lives would intersect again during the Holocaust.

When I was a little girl, I suffered from bronchial problems. *Bronchit* (bronchitis) was a very common word in my youth. I remember being treated with *bankes*, a traditional Ashkenazic Jewish folk remedy similar to "cupping," the ancient Chinese method believed to cleanse toxins and clear the lungs by encouraging circulation and removing blockages. The bankes were small glass cups that looked like miniature fish bowls. The treatment was administered by a *felsher*, a holistic practitioner. He started by dipping a large linen swab in rubbing alcohol and holding it over a flame until it caught fire. He placed the swab at the mouth of a banke to create a vacuum, then quickly applied the glass cup to the bare skin on my back. The bankes would leave great big pink circles on my skin that took a while to disappear. But I did get some relief.

In addition to my bronchial issues, I was very thin. It did not help that I was a very poor and picky eater. This greatly concerned my family so they were always trying to fatten me up, employing several different strategies.

Standing (l-r): Golda (director of the summer in Dumblė), Basia and her sister, Chaya Sarah Kamjonski, Eishyshok, late-1920s.

PERMISSION FOR USE GRANTED BY: YAFFA ELIACH SHTETL COLLECTION

One of these was to send me away in the summer to Dumblė, a popular vacation spot with resorts and summer camps. It was located not far from Eishyshok in an area of lush pine forests and freshwater lakes and rivers. I was too young for any of the area's formal summer camps, so I went instead to "fattening camp" at the home of Golda, an acquaintance of my mother's. Golda picked me up from my house in a horse and buggy, and we rode to her lovely *dacha*, her little cottage in the woods, for a session at her special camp. I was weighed like a little calf when I arrived at camp and again when I left. Success for Golda was measured in the number of kilos I gained.

Every day or maybe twice a day, I was forced to eat. Golda made *kashke marilke*, a concoction a bit like chocolate ganache, very rich and highly caloric. As far as I could tell, it was made with ten raw egg yolks, a quarter pound of sweet butter, half a cup of sugar and heaps of fresh cocoa. I ate it with a spoon until it was gone. I loved chocolate and sugar, so it was not a hardship. But the mass quantity made me feel a bit sick

Adolf Hitler

On January 30, 1933, Adolf Hitler, leader of the Nazi Party, was appointed Chancellor of Germany. A fascist dictator in the making, Hitler vowed to reverse Germany's humiliating defeat in World War I by rebuilding the military, reclaiming lost territory and restoring national pride. He quickly established a totalitarian Nazi regime fuelled by extreme nationalism, virulent racism and aggressive expansionism.

By the fall of 1939, Hitler stood poised to unleash a war that would engulf the world in a nightmare of hatred, bigotry, violence, slavery and mass murder.

Central to his ideology and war aims was Hitler's fanatical hatred of Jews, whom he scapegoated for Germany's problems. This anti-Semitism became the basis for the eventual genocide of six million Jews—a stain on the twentieth century that would come to be known as the Holocaust.

to my stomach. After eating the kashke marilke, I lay in a hammock strung between two trees to rest, swaying gently under the protection of their shade, surrounded by birds singing in the branches overhead.

The joy was overwhelming when I returned home from my time at camp a whopping two kilos heavier! I was so tiny that the weight gain was very visible, especially in my little hands, which were now much plumper. But inevitably I suffered another bronchial episode and as fast as I had gained the kilos I lost them.

It was decided that a stronger course of action was needed. I would have to drink pure cream. Papa, Mama, Bobe or Aunt Rivke took me to a nearby dairy, owned by Shael and Miriam Kaganowicz. I sat outside the Kaganowicz home with a bar of chocolate in one hand and a large glass of pure cream in the other. It was my job to finish both. I still love chocolate but I often wonder if my cholesterol issues today date back to those early "remedies."

The quiet focus on my health and the efforts to nurture my tiny frame were exceptions in the otherwise contented routine of my early life. I was blissfully sheltered by my family, the rhythms of our home, and the gentle day-to-day cadence of the shtetl. But beyond the borders of this serene existence, a storm was gathering and creeping toward us. A monumental shift was underway, orchestrated by a terrifying figure, still only a shadow in our world. But the shadow was growing. And his name—Adolf Hitler—would soon become known in every household and touch every life in Eishsyhok and beyond, including my family's.

I could hear the whispers of the adults. I was to young to grasp the details, but I could feel a quiet tension in our home and sense a change in the air. The summer I turned six, talk became action. I was too young to understand why. Was it truly a fortuitous job offer for Papa? Or was it a deeper instinct to move beyond danger and escape eastward to a city under a different, yet momentarily less menacing, authority. I will never know. But a decision had been made: We were leaving Eishyshok.

Lida

September 1939 – June 1941

Lida lies about forty-five kilometres from Eishyshok, in what is now western Belarus. Like Lithuania's rejection of Polish sovereignty over Eishyshok, the Soviet Union likewise denied Poland's claim to Lida and the surrounding eastern borderlands during the interwar years. Soviet authorities viewed Polish control as illegal. That was the rationale the USSR used in 1939—under the Molotov–Ribbentrop Pact—to justify regaining the region. By the time my family and I arrived in Lida, the city was once again under Soviet control. It was now part of the Belorussian Soviet Socialist Republic.

For most Jews in Lida, the Soviet takeover brought guarded relief, even cautious optimism. Of the three potential occupying forces—Germans, Poles and Soviets—the Russians were widely seen as the lesser evil. By then, the Nazis had already begun leaving a trail of destruction in western Poland following their early September invasion. Jewish refugees were fleeing eastward, driven by bitter memories and experiences of anti-Semitism in Poland, inflamed after Polish independence in 1918 by the nationalist slogan Polska dla Polaków—"Poland for the Poles."

Soviet rule, by contrast, was authoritarian but not explicitly anti-Semitic—at least at first. Communist ideology officially condemned anti-Semitism, and Jews were not systematically targeted in public life. Many welcomed the introduction of free healthcare, improved schools and access to government jobs. Some even held political positions.

The Molotov-Ribbentrop Pact

By summer 1939, relations between the Soviet Union and its former World War I allies—France and Great Britain—had frayed amid growing suspicion and conflicting strategies for confronting Nazi Germany. Hitler moved quickly to exploit the divide.

On August 23, 1939, Soviet foreign minister Vyacheslav Molotov and German foreign minister Joachim von Ribbentrop signed the Molotov-Ribbentrop Pact, a non-aggression treaty pledging that neither side would attack the other or support any third party that did. Secret protocols outlined how they would divide Eastern Europe—including the Baltic states, Finland and Poland. Crucially, the pact gave Hitler a free hand to invade Poland without fear of Soviet resistance.

Stalin's strategy could be summed up as "the enemy of my enemy is my friend." The pact was a ruthless but calculated gamble to secure strategic territory and buy time to prepare for the conflict with Germany he believed was inevitable.

On September 1, 1939, Germany invaded Poland from the west, igniting World War II. Seventeen days later, the Soviets invaded from the east, fanning the flames.

For many Jews, the new regime offered a sense of stability and opportunity. My mother's brother Chaim was among them. Already living in Lida, he worked as a foreman in a factory. He urged my father, Moshe—who spoke fluent Russian—to bring our family there. Papa took his advice, and Chaim helped him secure a good job at a city bank. I attended a Jewish day school, where I studied in Yiddish and began learning Russian. Slowly, we began to settle into our first experience of life under Soviet rule.

Uncle Chaim had always felt like a part of our home when we lived in Eishyshok because he was talked about so often. So, although I did not actually meet him until we moved to Lida, it felt very natural that my uncle now resided with us there. After the death of their father, and

Lida

Before World War II, the Jewish community of Lida thrived with a robust economy, vibrant scholarship and rich cultural and religious life.

Like much of the region, Lida changed hands multiple times in the early twentieth century, falling under the control of the Belorussian People's Republic, Lithuania, Poland, Nazi Germany and Soviet Russia.

On the eve of the war, the Jewish population numbered between eight thousand and eighty-five hundred, roughly 50–60% of the town's residents. More than 95% of Lida's Jews were murdered during the Holocaust.

Lida train station, 1939.
MUSEUM TOMATORUM / PUBLIC DOMAIN

Chaim Schuster (standing, far left) with a group of Bundists, Vilna, early 1920s.
COURTESY OF EVELYN KAHN

without a strong patriarch to guide them and keep them on a traditional Jewish path, my uncle and his older brother David had become rather rebellious. And secular.

As a teenager David had gone to school in Vilna. He was extremely bright and athletic, and he loved books as much as he loved soccer. I remember my grandmother once remarking that David's teachers praised him to the skies. They could not understand how he did so well in school given how much time he spent playing soccer. He had also become active in the General Jewish Labour Bund, a secular socialist Jewish workers' political movement that was especially active in Vilna. I imagine it held great appeal to him for its platform of brotherhood and equality. While still in his teens, David began to attend meetings of the local Bund and distribute leaflets for the cause. I do not know how many years he did this, but when he was about eighteen years old he was arrested and imprisoned in Vilna. When he was released, he went to the city of Vitebsk, in the Soviet Union, where he enrolled in university, became an agronomic engineer and got married. David was killed in Vitebsk during one of Stalin's purges.

Chaim followed in the footsteps of his older brother, including being imprisoned in Vilna. My best guess is he was incarcerated sometime in the mid- to late 1930s and it was related to his political activities. Like many Bundists, Chaim later joined the Communist Party. His political leanings and activities were not a secret in my family. I remember when we visited Uncle Henoch, my mother took along a lot of parcels, some of which were for my imprisoned uncle.

Lida was big and modern, a real city, with lovely architecture and buildings, clean paved streets, an airport and a beautiful train station. The Jews of Lida were more political and less religiously observant than those in our shtetl, but my family held fast to our lifestyle and maintained the same traditional Jewish home we had in Eishyshok. I remember, however, that we were more cautious about our Jewishness. When we lit candles for Shabbat we made sure to have the drapes drawn in our apartment. And when we were out in public we were careful to be discreet about being identifiably Jewish—or worse, middle class. Anti-Semitism may not have been part of Stalin's agenda but anti-capitalism was. The communists reviled the bourgeoisie as much as the Germans reviled the communists.

Somehow in April of 1940 our names were added to a list of capitalists marked for deportation to Siberia. It was thanks to Uncle Chaim's intervention that we were not deported. He managed, albeit with great difficulty, to get our names removed from that list.

We lived a very comfortable life in Lida. We had three apartments in a classical building. Rivke and her new husband from Zhetel, Shael Joselewitz, lived in one; my grandmother Hoda and Chaim lived in the second; and my parents and I lived in the third.

Hoda and Basia had given up their textile business before we left Eishyshok, but they had brought a healthy amount of the store's inventory with us. The fabrics were stored in the deep drawers of the large highboys in each of our three apartments. Our apartment had a good-sized living and dining room, with space for cushy sofas and oversized stuffed chairs. There was a colourful kilim rug on one wall, the flatwoven texture making the rug a pretty wall hanging. We also had several Biedermeier pieces, beautifully crafted German- and Austrian-inspired wooden furnishings that celebrated simple elegance and functionality in their design—very different from what we had in Eishyshok.

There was a lovely garden near our building where we took our meals in the summer. It had a beautiful lilac tree and my father would break off the purple flowers for me. He also bought me lilacs for my birthday, which I loved.

What I did not love was my mother making me eat soft-boiled eggs for breakfast. To this day I remove the membrane that holds the yolk to the egg white. Porridge was also not a favourite. But I loved brioche with unsalted butter, and still do. I ate it with rich hot chocolate. Divine.

My school was not far from the bank where Papa worked. My school uniform was a pleated navy skirt and long-sleeved white blouse. I also had a black pinafore with a ruffled trim over the armholes and along the stiff hemline. I wore it over my uniform to protect my clothes when I did art. I remember the school was very particular about our comportment, hygiene and appearance, and the teachers regularly checked my nails and hair. Papa used to pick me up after school and we walked home together. I loved walking home with him. One of my fondest memories is of my father taking me to my first marionette performance and being astonished that the little figures on the stage were just puppets.

I do not remember all our neighbours in Lida, but one of the apartments in our building was occupied by a lovely young Russian couple and their two daughters. One daughter, Svetlana, was the same age as me. Once, we were playing inside the foyer of our building with the front door unlocked. A man with a ruddy complexion, pocked skin, big, weeping blue eyes and slicked-back, ash-blond hair entered into the foyer. His face is as vivid to me now as it was then. I think he was drunk. He started to kiss Svetlana and then grabbed the back of my right shoulder. I wriggled away from him and took off up the stairs, shouting for our parents. By the time our mothers came down the man was gone.

Our house had many Russian visitors. One was a prosecutor, a friend of Uncle Chaim's. He wore many medals and there was always a lot of tension and a heightened sense of caution when he visited. My father did not like having the man in our home, and Papa's unease made me uncomfortable, too. But the prosecutor was an important communist and my father had to tolerate him—we could not do or say anything that might get us on the Russian's bad side and risk being sent away. Perhaps it was him that Chaim had contacted to intervene on our behalf to save us from deportation. It may explain in part my father's emotions and the overall strain in our home whenever the man was present. I have a recollection of him being the cause of a rare fight between my parents, but I never knew the details.

My family was constantly listening to the radio and were careful about what I was allowed to hear. I was far too young to understand that the world was at war, and I was also very sheltered. Nothing sad or serious was ever discussed in my presence. But children are perceptive, especially when grown-ups are trying to keep secrets. Conversations changed direction when I was around, and I caught glances and furtive exchanges between the adults. I absorbed things, even though I was not told directly.

We had lived in Lida for about a year and a half when our sojourn there came to an abrupt end in the summer of 1941. On June 22, barely three years into their agreement, Germany broke the Nazi-Soviet non-aggression pact and invaded Soviet-occupied Poland and the broader Soviet Union. The offensive, called Operation Barbarossa, quickly overwhelmed the Russians. They were caught completely off guard. And so were we.

Operation Barbarossa

The Nazis sought to create an Aryan empire and claimed they needed *Lebensraum*—"living space"—for the so-called German master race. Achieving this vision required the natural resources and territory of Eastern Europe. In a surprise attack known as Operation Barbarossa, more than three million German soldiers supported by thousands of tanks, artillery and aircraft crossed the Polish border into the Soviet Union. It was a textbook example of blitzkrieg, or lightning war—a rapid, overwhelming military offensive. To this day, it remains one of the largest and most devastating invasions in modern military history. Its date and time—4:00 a.m. on June 22—are memorialized in a popular Russian folk song, "The 22nd of June."

With planes already in the air and German soldiers on the march toward us, the Soviets broadcast an urgent bulletin spurring civilians to prepare for war. I remember helping my parents tape strips of kraft paper in giant Xs to our apartment windows.

We hoped this crude fortification would protect us from flying shards of glass, in case panes were shattered from the concussion of bomb blasts during an aerial assault. Similar Xs adorned the windows in all the neighbouring buildings. The authorities also ordered all members of the civil defence to report for duty. My father was a member. Before he left, he gave instructions to my mother, telling her we should run and seek shelter when the time came.

It came very quickly.

Very early one morning—while it was still dark outside—my family was awakened by the first sounds of war. The Germans had crossed into Belarus and within hours their Luftwaffe (German air force) planes arrived in Lida.

I do not remember Mama waking me. I just remember opening my eyes and seeing her next to my bed. "Chavale, mir muzn geyn (we have to go)," she said, as she helped me with my clothes and tying my sturdy lace-ups. Barely had she finished when she grabbed my hand and we raced with my grandmother and my aunt Rivke through the hallway, down the stairs and out of our building—into pandemonium. The German invasion of Lida was playing out before our eyes. A live-action war film come to life.

My senses were on overload. The sights, smells and sounds are as fresh now as they were then. I had never seen so many people, masses of them heading every which way. My heart was beating fast and I felt nauseous. We joined a crush of people streaming away from the city centre, seeking shelter wherever they could find it.

"Leyf schnell, Chavale. Bleib nit shteyn (Run fast, Chavale. Don't slow down)," urged my mother as we followed the masses toward the edge of town. I was flanked by her and Bobe, each holding one of my small hands fast in one of theirs. As we raced across the cobbled street—right, left, straight—we could hear the drone of low-flying aircraft approach overhead. We looked up to see scores of Luftwaffe planes sweeping through the sky, blocking out the sun. The hum of their heavy engines competed with the cacophony of sounds in the street. The noise was deafening. The sky was turning ashen, the air smelled of burning wood and we could see the glow of fires in the distance at the Lida airfield. We barely had time to register the aircraft when a whistling-buzzing sound tore through the air and bullets strafed the ground around us.

Bombs followed the shooting. The planes flew so low over us that I imagined the Luftwaffe pilots could see us. I was sure they were going to take aim directly at our little quartet, which was still in the open racing for cover. The bullets and bombs missed us. But I could hear people falling behind us. It was a chilling feeling. We took cover in a little orchard just as the planes circled back for another pass. Cowering together, we watched as a Luftwaffe plane caught up to a Soviet plane and started shooting at it. The Soviet was hit and Mama, Bobe, Rivke and I gasped as it fell to earth and burst into flames. It was a crushing blow. We were all in tears.

The aerial assault lasted many hours. When it was over, the air raid siren sounded the "all clear." The four of us left our shelter in the trees and entered into a hellscape. The destruction was beyond anything we could imagine. Buildings bombed out. Craters opened in the street. Human carnage. Fires burned all around and thick grey smoke filled the air. I choked and coughed as we made our way home to our apartment.

Thankfully, our building was not hit. But our apartment had been damaged. My father was waiting for us. Around him the windows were caved in and walls torn out. Papa was sitting in a chair, with his hands folded in his lap. I picked up on his body language. There was fear and resignation. It was a new sensation for me to see Papa defeated. It unsettled me. I did not like it.

We barely had time to recover from the bombing when two days later we heard loud voices on the stairs and two uniformed men burst into our apartment. The *Wehrmacht* (armed forces of Nazi Germany) had arrived in Lida between June 25 and June 27, and now two of their soldiers were standing in our living room.

They grabbed my father roughly by the lapels. "Are there any weapons or spies here?" barked one of them.

Papa was very frightened but answered. "No, I do not own any guns. I am a volunteer with the civil defence."

The soldiers would not be swayed. Telling us not to move, they went off to search our home. "Remember," said the same soldier, "if I find anything here, your life will not be worth living. I will kill you."

A few minutes later, the soldiers returned to the salon, one of them brandishing a gun. Unbeknownst to us, Uncle Chaim had hidden his revolver under his mattress. The soldier waved my uncle's gun at my father and moved menacingly toward him. "I knew you were a spy," he declared. "I am going to shoot you now," and he pointed the gun at my father's groin.

Bobe Hoda, Basia, Rivke and I fell to our knees, tearfully begging the soldiers to let my father live. My mother and grandmother explained that we had all been out of the house trying to escape the bombs—anyone could have come into our apartment and hidden the gun while we were out. One of the soldiers started to soften up. "You deserve to die," he told my father. "But I will spare your life."

My quick-thinking grandmother immediately went over to the highboy with the fabrics and opened all the drawers. "Please, take anything you want. Anything we have," said Bobe Hoda. "Just please do not take the child's father. He is the only male member of the family."

The soldier softened further. He told us he was a *Volksdeutsche*, one of the ethnic Germans born or living outside Germany who did not hold German citizenship. He had been conscripted from Czechoslovakia into the Wehrmacht, leaving behind his poor suffering mother. The soldier walked over to the dresser, looked at the selection of fabrics and chose a bolt. I can still see it: a beautiful navy-blue shantung silk with large white polka dots.

"I would like you to have this for your mother," my grandmother told him, pressing the fabric into his hands. She then blessed him to the skies and praised his mother for raising such a wonderful son. His companion indicated he wanted nothing. Then, as though it was the most natural thing in the world, my grandmother made tea and served cake. I have a vivid memory of the soldiers making us drink the tea first for fear it was poisoned. When our impromptu "tea party" was over, the soldiers rose to leave. Our family bowed deferentially to the men as they moved toward the door, where they stopped to tell us how lucky we were to have engaged with them and not with the SS. And with that, they were gone.

The infantry soldiers who invaded our home were the spearhead of the Wehrmacht. In the days that followed, more troops arrived in Lida, including units from Nazi paramilitary organizations. Chief among them was the machinery of mass murder: the *Waffen-SS* (armed branch of the SS or *Schutzstaffel*); the *Einsatzgruppen* (mobile death squads) and their smaller killing units, the *Einsatzkommandos*; and the Gestapo, the secret police.

In simple terms, the SS enforced Nazi racial policy. The Einsatzgruppen and Einsatzkommandos hunted down and murdered the "undesirables," primarily Jews, but also other groups such as Communists and Roma (Gypsies). The Gestapo, with help of local collaborators, rooted them out.

The Final Solution

Endlösung der Judenfrage, meaning "Final Solution to the Jewish Question," was the Nazi regime's term for its plan to exterminate the Jewish people. What began as policies to drive Jews from Germany and its territories—to make them Judenrein ("cleansed of Jews")—escalated into systematic mass murder in 1941. The "Final Solution" was formalized at the Wannsee Conference in January 1942, where Nazi leaders coordinated the blueprint for the machinery of genocide across Europe. Through pogroms, ghettos, mass shootings and industrialized killing in extermination camps, nearly two-thirds of Europe's Jews were murdered—including more than 90% of the Jewish populations of Poland and Lithuania.

Carrying out the "Final Solution"—the Nazis' plan to eradicate all Jews from Europe—required a vast and coordinated workforce, all in service of cleansing the so-called *Volkskörper* (national body) of what they saw as an "infection": the Jewish people.

I am not sure we could have wrapped our minds around the magnitude of the forces aligned against us had we even known the scale and scope of the Nazi's master plan. I am not sure anyone could have. It was massive. Sophisticated. And merciless. What my parents did comprehend without any doubt was that the terrifying incident in our apartment and the arrival of the Nazi forces in Lida meant a new reality. "Moshe, the time has come when you must leave Lida.

You cannot be exposed again," said my grandmother to my father. "We must all go to a place that is smaller and more secure." And quickly.

Contact was made with the family of Rivke's new husband, Shael Joselewitz, in Zhetel, fifty kilometres to the south of Lida, and preparations were made for us to move there. Chaim could not help us. He and Shael had been forcibly conscripted into the Soviet Red Army. The Soviet military had suffered catastrophic losses during Operation Barbarossa. (I read after the war that close to a million Soviet soldiers died, were injured or captured in the first month after the German invasion.) As a result, they began grabbing up men of military age to try and reinforce Soviet lines.

My father, mother and grandmother managed to secure a covered wagon with two horses. Hoda announced that she would remain behind to dispose of our things and would meet up with us later. Rivke stayed to help her. We kissed them goodbye, and then Papa, Mama and I climbed into the wagon and left. We travelled through the night, arriving in Zhetel sometime in the pre-dawn hours on the morning of the following day. My best guess is that we arrived around the same time as the Germans, perhaps one day before. We stayed briefly with the Joselewitz family, then moved to a duplex of our own and anxiously awaited the arrival of my grandmother and aunt.

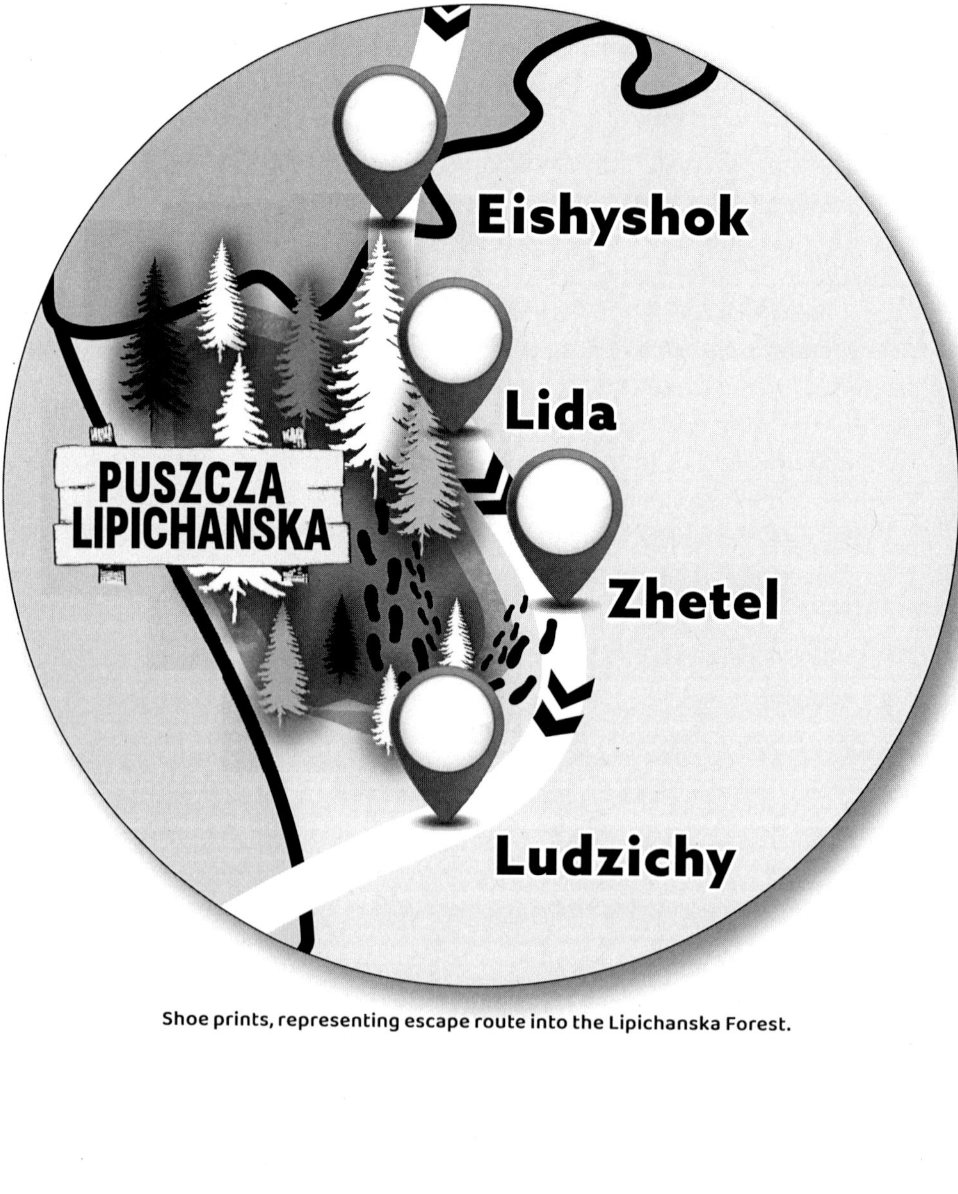

Shoe prints, representing escape route into the Lipichanska Forest.

PART TWO
On the Run

Zhetel

June 1941 – February 1942

Zhetel is a small town about 50KM south of Lida.

We were one family among many hundreds of refugees from nearby towns who fled there seeking a safe haven that June. But Zhetel would prove exactly the opposite.

Lida had given me an up close and personal taste of German infantry soldiers. But it was in Zhetel that my family and I would experience the true depths of the capacity for inhumanity of individuals to their fellow human beings. When we first arrived, we were all still somewhat naïve to the insidious and deadly methods of the SS, a self-proclaimed "racially elite" special police force. The loss of our innocence did not take long.

Main street, Zhetel, c. 1930s.
PERMISSION FOR USE GRANTED BY: TAMARA VERSHITSKAYA, THE TOGETHER PLAN, BELARUS, FROM HER PRIVATE COLLECTION.

It began with the imposition of a host of decrees. First, a curfew. Any Jew caught outside their home after curfew was shot. The SS mandated that we wear the yellow Star of David patch on the front and back of our clothing. We were prohibited from using public transportation or walking on sidewalks. Jews could not gather in groups. The punishment for violating any of the rules was death. Already, stories were being shared by Jews arriving from neighbouring towns where the SS, with their Belorussian and Polish collaborators, tortured Jews and murdered them in cold blood. All the edicts were part of the Nazi agenda to methodically diminish us and break our spirit. Little did we know that these directives would prove to be minor inconveniences relative to those to come.

Zhetel

Before World War II, Zhetel was a vibrant centre of Jewish life. The town had four Jewish schools, several houses of worship and a rich cultural scene that included a theatre, Jewish newspapers and numerous youth organizations representing the full spectrum of Zionist and political movements of the time. At the outbreak of the war, Zhetel was home to around thirty-five hundred Jews, who made up roughly three-quarters of the town's population. By 1941, that number had grown to an estimated forty-five hundred as refugees arrived from surrounding villages to escape Nazi roundups. At the time, Zhetel was part of the Soviet Union. Today it is known as Dzyatlava, in independent Belarus. No Jews live there now.

Our real nightmare began at 4:00 a.m. on July 23, 1941—the same hour the Germans had invaded the Soviet Union almost one month earlier. It is a day that is seared into my memory.

"Chavale, shtei uf (wake up)," my mother said, as she nudged me from my slumber.

"Mama, es iz finzter, far vos darf ich ufshtein (it's still dark out, why do I have to get up?)," I told her, as I tried to burrow under my blanket.

"Kum, Chavale, mir muzn leifen shnell (Come, Chavale, we have to run quickly)," she said, as she helped me into the long-sleeved, medium-weight navy wool dress with a white baby collar that had become my uniform in the ghetto.

Judenräte (Jewish Councils)

Judenräte (Jewish Councils) were administrative bodies established in ghettos throughout Nazi-occupied Eastern Europe. Made up of local Jewish leaders—often community elders, professionals or rabbis—these councils were appointed by the Nazis and forced to serve as intermediaries between the German authorities and the Jewish population. The Nazis used the Judenräte to divide, destabilize and dominate the Jews, all part of facilitating the Final Solution. The councils carried out duties such as maintaining order in the ghettos, organizing food distribution, collecting valuables, enforcing curfews and, most painfully, compiling lists of Jews for forced labour and deportation.

I became conscious of noise outside. Shouts. Raised voices. I wanted to ask my mother what was happening, but I could tell there was no time for explanations. I was still rubbing the sleep from my eyes when Mama, Papa and I hastened from our house.

The whole ghetto was awake, twelve hundred Jews roused from their beds in the early morning hours and forced from their homes by harsh knocks and rifle shots from the SS and their local Belorussian proxies. Men, women and sleepy children were being herded toward the ghetto's marketplace. My parents each held one of my small hands tucked securely into one of theirs as we joined the crowd and made our way slowly along the packed streets.

The SS had issued a summons through the Judenrat, the Jewish Council, that all able-bodied Jewish men aged sixteen to sixty were to report to the marketplace, in the centre of Zhetel. They were needed for a work detail outside the ghetto. Each man was to bring with him provisions for three days. No one was to remain at home. Any man who did not report endangered not only his life but also the lives of all the members of his family.

A chill of foreboding ran up my spine as we arrived at the marketplace and I took in the scores of armed men in an assortment of uniforms and high black leather jackboots. The men looked like predatory animals. I knew they were not all German, but I was too young then to distinguish who was who. It was not until much later, after reading survivor testimonies, that I understood the guards in the square that day were a mix of Gestapo, SS Einsatzkommandos, Belorussian auxiliary police and Nazi collaborators. They shouted and pushed, trampling or hitting anyone who did not move fast enough. This seemed to tickle our "audience," Zheteler spectators gathered on the periphery, laughing at the show. Once we were assembled, an officer announced that those whose names he was about to call should step forward.

Unbeknownst to us, gatherings just like this were happening or had happened in other ghettos across Eastern Europe, with the same objective: to round up and eliminate the ghetto's intelligentsia—Jewish thinkers, leaders and potential fighters—who could organize resistance and revolt. Nazi collaborators and locals in Zhetel had obligingly assisted in compiling a list of names of Zhetel's professionals for the Gestapo. Doctors, teachers, lawyers, businessmen, shopkeepers, students, rabbis—anyone who might be able to influence or organize the ghetto's Jews against the Nazis.

One by one, Zhetel's best and brightest were separated from the group, including Motl Bielski, the teacher from Zhetel who used to board with us in Eishyshok, and Shifra Dunetz, a nurse with socialist leanings and the only woman among them. I could sense the tension in the air build as each name was called. They said goodbye to loved ones, were walked to a small table to register and were then photographed. Nothing to fear. The whole thing looked very innocent. When it was done, the group was led under guard across the square, loaded into military trucks and driven away.

After the last name on the list was called, the SS officer appealed to the remaining men in the crowd to volunteer for the work detail. It would only be for a few days. It was light work, he assured them.

It was then that my father made a fateful decision. He would volunteer. Moshe's name had not been called. How could it have been? Our family were newly arrived refugees. No one would have known Moshe Landsman, let alone that he was an educated professional, certainly not those who had compiled the list. But there he was now, volunteering to go.

I can only surmise that my father assumed it was better to volunteer than to be forcibly seized. Papa would have known about the *scheinen*, the little paper passes handed out by the Germans to those deemed to have useful skills, such as skilled labourers and tradespeople. The scheinen protected the workers as well as their families from being rounded up. But my father knew he'd never qualify as a labourer and secure a pass for us. His soft accountant's hands gave him away. Perhaps, by volunteering now he had a chance to survive.

Papa had barely picked me up when—whack!—I was struck on the back of my small shoulders by hard rifle butts. Message delivered. My father's embrace was lasting too long. Papa put me down carefully next to my mother, eyeing the two German soldiers and their rifles with caution. I saw pain in my father's eyes. I knew he wished the blows had landed on his own shoulders instead of mine.

Mama passed Papa the small burlap sack with the three-day provisions she had been instructed to bring with us. I remember she had packed a little bread and salt. I think she may have added a few potatoes, a few eggs. Maybe an apple. I had no time to wonder if it would be enough to sustain my father. The nasty men with the rifles were already taking my papa away.

Mama was crying now. I was inconsolable. It was one of the few occasions I can recall either of us giving in to tears during the Holocaust. We watched in misery as Papa climbed into the back of a truck and was driven away. I never saw my father again.

The day's ordeal continued for several more hours. When it was over, Mama took my hand, kissed me gently and said, "Kum mayn kind, es is tzayt tsu geyn aheim yetzt (Come my child, it is time to go home now)."

When three days had come and gone and the men had not returned, the families began to worry. Rumours abounded. The women were told the men had been killed in ditches outside town. Or the men had been gathered in nearby Slonim, and when that shtetl's inhabitants were massacred, so were our men. We were beside ourselves. The only people who consoled us were the others whose fathers, husbands, uncles, grandfathers and sons had been taken.

At some point my mother, along with a small delegation of women whose men had been taken, set out to search for them. The German army was still advancing along the roadways, so the women walked in the culverts along the sides of the roads. The women sought out farmers along the way who might be able to shed light on the mystery of the disappearance of their men. They were told everything except the truth. But the truth has a way of not staying buried. And my mother eventually learned the fate of my father and the rest.

Two days after the men were taken away, SS Einsatzgruppen forced them to dig their own graves before shooting my father and the others in a forest near Novogrudek, a town about twenty-five kilometres from Zhetl. They were buried in a communal ditch there.

Mama kept this information from me. She thought I would feel more secure if I believed there was someone who could care for me in case something happened to her. I was a very pampered child with no street smarts. It would have been highly unlikely that I could have survived on my own, with nothing more than a fantasy that I might be reunited with my father. However, my very wise mother had given me an important survival tool that would sustain me throughout the war. She gave me hope. The great English philosopher John Milton said the mind can make heaven or hell. The hope my mother instilled in me then allowed me to make heaven while I went through hell.

Bobe Hoda was devastated when she arrived in Zhetel soon after and learned that Moshe had been taken away. She was convinced that had she been with us she could have persuaded him to go into hiding and not to go to the roundup.

Shortly after Papa was taken, we were reunited with Uncle Chaim. He had escaped from a German POW camp and made his way hundreds of kilometres back to us, barely making it out of Lida ahead of the Germans—where he went first to look for us—then tracking us to Zhetel. Escaping from the camp was proof enough of his boldness and courage. But it was his ingenuity that truly knew no bounds. He travelled disguised as a Lipka Tatar peasant from Lithuania. Lipka Tatars are Turkic Muslims, and as such, they are circumcised. And as an officer in the Russian army, Uncle Chaim's full head of wavy black hair did not give him away as a POW since only regular enlisted soldiers had buzz cuts.

How my grandmother embraced her son and how they both cried like children! Our joy in having him back on the heels of losing Papa was indescribable. Chaim lovingly filled the void left by my father. My favourite place to sit was in his lap. Chaim was my rock. And Bobe Hoda's. He could do no wrong in her eyes. She completely indulged him.

Dubl

My uncle had long ago abandoned keeping kosher and thought nothing of bringing home *traif*, non-kosher food. In addition to smuggling in bread and potatoes from local farms, he would also occasionally bring home lard when he visited us. Hoda would turn a blind eye to this egregious transgression, pretending not to notice when he "hid" the lard in the little *dubl*, Yiddish for "double," a small hinged ventilation window within a larger one. It was their little game. My uncle and I had one of our own.

Uncle Chaim loved to tease me with his prized stash. Out of sight of my bobe, he would hold the lard up to my nose and say in his teasing tone, "Chavale, nem a shtikel, es iz zeyer geshmak (have a bit, it's delicious)." Bobe Hoda's concession to her son and his lard spoke volumes of her love for him. Even in the ghetto, my grandmother was very devout and kept a kosher home. Remarkably, when many of us lapsed in our observance of *kashrut* (Jewish dietary laws) to sustain our lives during the war, my bobe never lapsed in hers.

Four months after the murder of my father, the ripples of change and disquiet in Zhetel grew stronger. On November 28, 1941, the Germans decreed that we had to deliver all our valuables, such as money, gold, silver and jewellery, to Gestapo headquarters. The impact of this decree and the ones which followed was not lost on us. Being stripped of precious goods meant being stripped of commodities we could trade for basic food and clothing. But non-compliance was not an option.

The Germans were fond of driving this home to us with cruel lessons, as was the case of Liba Gertzovsky. She showed up at the headquarters with her possessions and was told to turn out her coat pockets. One of the German gendarmes had secretly put two rings in her pocket and "caught" her in her "lie," accusing her of not relinquishing everything when they searched her. She was taken to the centre of town and shot dead as an example to the rest of us.

The murder happened so fast. I was frozen in place, in complete shock and disbelief. My mother grabbed my shoulders and turned me quickly into her body. I was eight years old and could not comprehend what I had seen. After the shock came numbness; once that wore off, reality hit. And so did the tears. But tears were a luxury we couldn't afford. There was no room for hysteria. It was a struggle not to show fear when every nerve in my body was vibrating with it. I could barely breathe. I felt empty and yet I wanted to vomit. But I would be damned before I showed hints of victimhood or weakness to the murderers. And so would the rest of us. We remained outwardly neutral in their presence and fought silently within to stay resolute. We could not lose our faith. We could not lose our courage. We needed to remain strong for the adversities to come. I believe this was the event when I first realized that to stay strong, I would have to conquer my fear—and cling to hope.

On February 22, 1942, the Gestapo posted decrees around the city announcing that all the Jews in Zhetel needed to leave their homes and move into a ghetto. I am not sure how many hours we were given to prepare and get organized. I have read different survivor accounts that suggest anywhere from one hour to twelve. I am inclined toward the former or somewhat closer to that shorter window. In the end it is a minor detail. There would never have been enough time.

It was not easy to decide what to take and what to leave behind. My mother and Bobe still had some of the fabrics left from those they had managed to bring from Lida. They had been using them to barter for food and necessities. But they knew they could no longer use them as currency once we entered the ghetto. Our trading days were over.

To leave the ghetto without permission was punishable by death. We could be shot for trying to get food from the gentiles. We could be shot for just talking to them. Bobe Hoda and Mama gave the remaining cloth to Uncle Chaim, who gave it to a gentile acquaintance of his to safeguard for us, a security deposit on the man's help in the future.

My family and I walked, step by step, in the middle of the road past the homes and watchful eyes of our gentile neighbours to our new living accommodations. We were a sad parade of Jews, schlepping whatever meagre belongings we could carry.

Novogrudek Street, Zhetel, 1940s.

PERMISSION FOR USE GRANTED BY: TAMARA VERSHITSKAYA, THE TOGETHER PLAN, BELARUS, FROM HER PRIVATE COLLECTION.

Zhetel markeptlace, 1940.
PERMISSION FOR USE GRANTED BY: TAMARA VERSHITSKAYA, THE TOGETHER PLAN, BELARUS, FROM HER PRIVATE COLLECTION.

Zhetel Ghetto

February 1942 – August 1942

The Zhetel ghetto was roughly a mile long and ten blocks square for approximatly 5,000 Jews.

It was circumscribed by several streets, including Lisagura and part of Slonim Street until Shushne. The area was located near the largest of the town's three synagogues and one of the two Jewish day schools. The ghetto was surrounded in part by a wood fence with barbed wire at the top. The Germans had appropriated the homes within the confines of the ghetto and stripped them of their comfortable furnishings. Regular beds were replaced by double and triple bunk beds to accommodate many families together in homes previously occupied by just one family.

In the beginning, life in the Zhetel ghetto was tolerable for us. Or maybe just for me. At least that is how I remember it. I know we were crowded together with strangers in deplorable conditions. I know there were food shortages and sanitation challenges. I know there was hunger and deprivation. But, remarkably, I do not recall suffering in those early days, probably due to a combination of the extraordinary strength of my mother and grandmother, the near impenetrable force field of protection they conjured around me, and my own magical thinking. My defences were strong. Mama and Bobe were like steel. The stoicism they modelled for me became part of my own self.

On April 29, 1942, barely two months after we had moved into the ghetto, the Germans arrested the members of the Judenrat. The following day, April 30, we were roused before dawn by the sounds of gunfire, barking dogs and yelling. "Juden raus, Juden raus (Jews out, Jews out)!"

came the shouts as men rained blows on windows and doors across the ghetto. The first liquidation (forced emptying of the ghetto) had begun.

The SS, together with the assistance of the Belorussian auxiliary police and, probably, helpful eager locals from neighbouring towns, rousted us from our homes. The local militia were especially brutal. They had a propensity for drunkenness and undisciplined behaviour that even the Germans found reprehensible. The soldiers and guards, aided by their vicious dogs, forced us into the street. They herded us together into a human column and marched us toward the old cemetery, which was located within the ghetto. Although I do not remember witnessing it, I learned later that some Jews who did not leave their homes fast enough or were slow to obey orders were kicked and beaten. Others were shot.

My own memory of the procession along the street is of being corralled into a narrow funnel and of feeling smothered by the crush of human bodies around me. I remember telling my mother I could not breathe. I was worried I might pass out and be trampled. People were on top of one another—on top of me—crying and tearing their hair out. I wanted Mama to pick me up, but it was impossible. We were compressed like livestock in a cattle chute. I just held onto Mama's hand and prayed that mine would not slip out of hers.

"Zei dershtikin mir, Mama (They're suffocating me, Mother)," I called out to my mother.

She bent down close to me and I will never forget her tearful words. "Mayn kind, es iz beser men zol dir dershtikn eyder mayne oygn zoln zen vi men shist dir (My child, it is better that you should suffocate here than my eyes should witness you being murdered)."

I took in what she said and then simply asked and asked my mother whether it hurt to die. She assured me it was a peaceful experience. "Neyn mayn kind, es iz vey a feygele, git a brum (No my child, it is like a chirp of a bird)."

Her answer quieted my fears and calmed me. I was never afraid of death from that moment on. I never remember feeling despair. On the contrary, I was exceptionally calm and clear throughout the nightmare to come. The whole situation seemed rather basic and simple to my young mind. I simply could not conceive of myself as a dead person, like poor Liba Gertzovsky. I was alive.

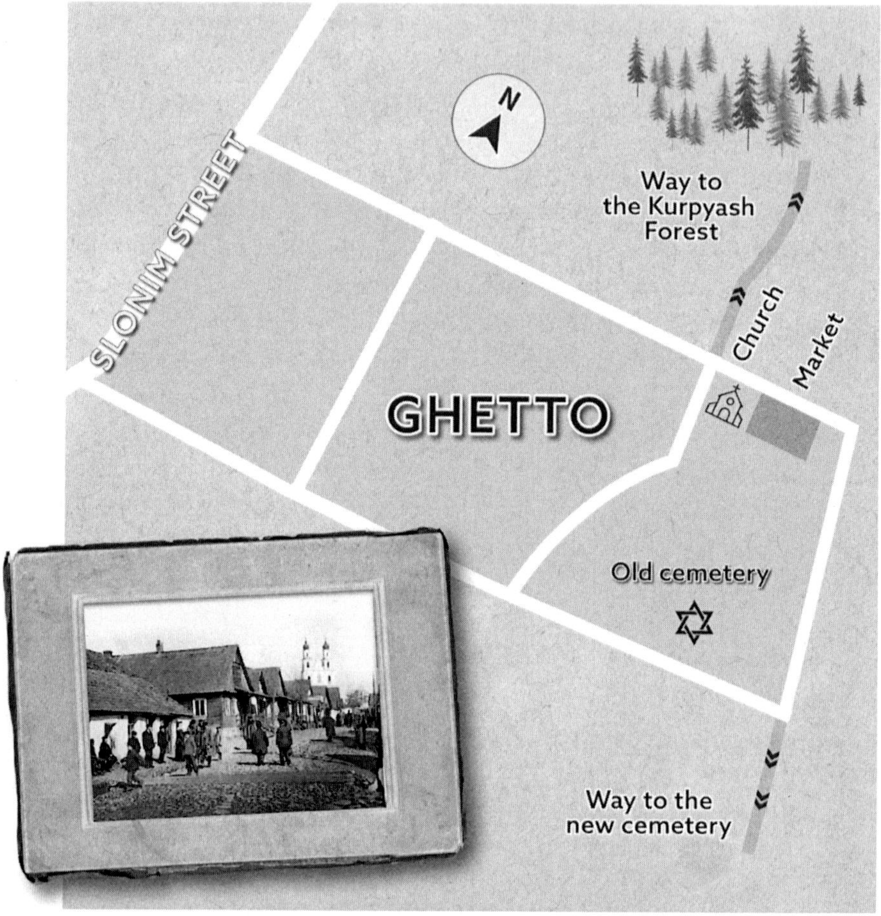

Slonim Street and map of Zhetel Ghetto, 1942.
PERMISSION FOR USE GRANTED BY: TAMARA VERSHITSKAYA, THE TOGETHER PLAN, BELARUS, FROM HER PRIVATE COLLECTION.FROM HER PRIVATE COLLECTION.

We entered the Jewish cemetery within the ghetto. I could see open trucks and guards surrounding every side of the area. As I processed the scene, I could not figure out exactly what was going to happen, but I knew it would be horrible. And with that knowledge came an unexpected sense of resignation and acceptance. I was not afraid of whatever was to come.

The Nazi SS and Belorussians forced us into lines to be sorted. I learned as an adult from other survivor memoirs that the selection was overseen by Novogrudek's regional commander, Gebietskommissar Wilhelm Traub. He indicated with the wave of his finger to which side of the square each of us should be sent. With a single gesture he decided who would live and who would die that day. I recall being sorted but do not recall to which side we were sent. I just remember all the men without disabilities and those with the right scheinen in one group and us in the other. Our group was made up of women and children, older adults, frail men and people of all ages with disabilities. We were to be loaded onto trucks.

I walked with my mother to our transport. My mother held my right hand and as I raised my right foot to climb into the back of a truck, she yanked me by my arm so hard I thought she would break it. She grabbed me and we ran together toward a group of skilled workers waiting on the left side of the square. One of the men in that group was a *blekher*, a sheet metal worker. He started hollering to the guards that we were part of his family and reached out for my mother. The guards just laughed, but they let Mama and me go to him. We started to cry, and people in the group started to cry with us. But where was Bobe Hoda?

"I lost Hoda," said my mother. Another man in the group told her, "Look, Bashke, your mother is doing what you did. She's running. They're hitting her but she's running."

Blows were raining upon my bobe and we watched with growing apprehension as she raced toward us. I think the only reason the soldiers did not kill her is because in that crowded square, had they shot at her they risked killing one of their own. And besides, they knew the game. If they did not get her this time, they would get her the next. When the blekher asked her later how she had run so fast, Bobe said she was spurred on by a single hope—she did not want to be buried in an anonymous ditch. She wanted a proper Jewish burial in a Jewish cemetery. I wonder how she thought that might have been remotely possible under the circumstances. But that hope was enough to give her the speed she needed to rejoin us.

As we headed back to the ghetto, we registered bodies in the marketplace. I saw enough blood that day to last a lifetime. But I would see a lot more.

I have a memory of my mother fasting on the day of the liquidation. It was the custom in our family to mark the *yahrzeit* (anniversary of death) of a loved one by fasting on the anniversary of his or her death.

And Basia was very faithful to this tradition. I vividly recall that after the selection we went to someone's home, and a man offered my mother some water, which she declined. She said that she was fasting in memory of her father, a custom she had been observing since the age of ten. She told the man that she attributed the miracle of our salvation that day to her father and that her fast had been in his merit.

A total of twelve hundred Jews who had been at the cemetery that day were selected to die. They were marched to the Kurpyash forest, about four kilometres south of Zhetel, where they were forced by the SS to dig large pits, which would be used as mass graves. When the graves were done, the Jews were separated into groups of twenty, taken to the pits and shot by SS Einsatzkommandos. Those Jews who had not been fated to die in the massacre that day were returned to the ghetto. It was reduced in size and we were forced to live in even tighter quarters. I imagine it must have been difficult for the Zhetelers to have us forcibly accommodated in their homes. But it was certainly no less difficult for us.

Our new quarters were very crowded. I think we were approximately thirty people in total in our house, with eight to ten people to a room. I remember we lived with one other family in the same room. The accommodations were filthy, with no indoor toilet facilities or running water. An outhouse served the needs of all the residents. People fought. Lice were everywhere, contributing to illnesses and death. We rationed our food as best we could and somehow Bobe and Mama would make a few potatoes and a little flour last a few weeks instead of a few days. But we were hungry.

Life became more and more unbearable and desperate. People were starving and disease was rampant. Fear was everywhere. Secure hiding places became as necessary as food. Maybe more so. Many homes had secret bunkers or concealed hiding spaces. Uncle Shael's did. He and Aunt Rivke hid in their home during the first liquidation. Our new accommodations had a secret hiding place, called a *skhron* in Russian.

After the first liquidation, Uncle Chaim had fled to the forest. He had joined the partisans and was very anxious to take us all out of the ghetto to join him. Anticipating the second liquidation, my uncle sent Basia a message advising her that he was going to come and rescue

Jewish partisans (standing l-r): Pietka, Benjamin, and Leibke (Leon Kahn), c. 1944.
COURTESY OF EVELYN KAHN

all of us. But I had contracted scarlet fever, putting a halt to his plans. We would have to wait. The doctor told my mother it was ill-advised to move me to the forest, as the conditions there would not be conducive to my recovery. Neither, however, were the conditions at home.

Several of our housemates had made it clear to my mother that she needed to remove me from our home lest I infect them and their children with scarlet fever. Their hostility was so intense that Mama was forced to move me. The only place she could think of where I could convalesce in relative safety was the local sanitarium. So, Mama wrapped me in a blanket and carried me there. I remember the patients there screaming and many running

The Partisans

The Soviet partisans were a diverse and often uneasy mix of Red Army remnants, communists, former Soviet political prisoners, and escapees from German POW camps. This group also contained renegades and criminals who exploited their partisan status to persecute Jews. The Jewish partisans, in contrast, were refugees from local villages, survivors of ghettos, and escapees from labour and concentration camps.

The Soviets fought the Germans for the survival of Mother Russia. The Jews fought for their very survival—for themselves, for all those still trapped in the ghettos, and to avenge those who had already been murdered.

around half-naked. Little did the other residents in our house know at the time that there was a far deadlier threat to their lives than I. The second liquidation was nearly upon us.

It began on Thursday, August 6, 1942, and lasted for three days. This was the final liquidation and it would mark the end of the Zhetel ghetto. Like the first liquidation, this one also began with an order for us all to report to the marketplace. Then came the gunfire. My mother and I heard the shots from the institution. They sounded like they were coming from every direction. Mama knew in an instant what was happening. She immediately grabbed me, wrapped me in a blanket and ran with me in her arms back to our home. It was quite a distance.

The house was nearly deserted. Basia knew something was not right. Only Bobe and one other family from Zhetel—a woman around my bobe's age and her two children, a boy and a girl in their twenties—were there. All the rest of the residents had gone to the marketplace as ordered. Everyone who went was taken away to the new Jewish cemetery on the southern edge of the town and murdered that day—three thousand innocent souls.

Basia had sworn that she would never step into the marketplace again. It was instant death. We decided to take our chances at home in our skhron. However, the mother and her two children told Bobe and Mama they would not allow me into the skhron because I was still ill. There was no way my grandmother and mother were going to let this family determine the fate of ours. My mother and grandmother told the mother and her children they were selfish. They assured the woman and her children that I was no longer a risk; I was just weak. My mother and grandmother further supported their case by telling the family that we were all probably doomed anyway, like everyone in the marketplace. I guess the truth of that finally sank in. It was time to hide.

Our skhron was quite long. It reached underneath the rear of the house and extended under the backyard to the garden, where vegetables grew over it. Access to the skhron was through a hidden opening in the kitchen floor, under a large tarnished copper barrel with a lid, called a *kessel*, which was used to boil water for household needs, including laundry. Getting into the skhron meant moving the

Illustration based on Evelyn's recollection of her family's skhron in the Zhetel Ghetto.

heavy kessel. Not an easy task. Mama and the twenty-something-year-old young man either tipped it or just slid it over a bit so the access was revealed. It was hard work. I remember I had to be lifted down through the opening into the crude space beneath the floor. When the rest of our little group had squeezed through and we were all settled inside the skhron, Mama and the young man somehow manoeuvred the kessel back exactly into its place, so the opening was completely camouflaged.

There was enough room to accommodate more than just the six of us, but the ceiling was very low, and we had to crawl on our hands and knees. I was only nine years old, but I could not sit up straight inside our bunker. I cannot imagine how challenging this was for Mama, who was tall. She and Bobe had prepared limited stores of food and water in the skhron, as well as some blankets and heavy grey woollen socks with a white cuff and a thin red stripe across the top. It was a pity we had no earplugs. The sounds around us were terrifying. We heard a lot of shooting, followed by screaming and crying as occupied bunkers were discovered and grenades were thrown into hiding spots. We were sure it was just a matter of time until it was our turn. We heard soldiers and their henchmen ransacking our home, shouting and cursing "Bloody, bastards. Dirty Jews. We know there is a hideout right here and we'll find you. We're coming after you."

There was very little circulation in the space and the air felt very heavy. I recall there was an aluminum pail for our waste, but my olfactory memory has been wiped away. I slept a lot as my body recovered. I had no sense of time. My mother had a thermometer and regularly took my temperature. Everyone was silent lest we be heard by passing neighbours or soldiers. I remember the other family had a very negative attitude. I could sense a lot of tension, and I remember whispered arguments. Bobe and Mama did their best to keep our spirits up as they hoped for a miracle. My strongest recollection of that time is my fear of being captured alive and tortured.

We stayed in the bunker for seven days and seven nights. At some point, my grandmother suddenly held her chest, and I could see she was in great pain. But she did not cry out. It was her first attack of angina. Bobe Hoda had wells of strength like no one else. She was not going to die in that dark place. She willed herself to bear the pain.

On the seventh day of hiding, we noted that it had grown very quiet outside. Our enemies had finally moved on and we needed to as well. It was time to escape. But first we needed to get out of the skhron.

Coming out of our bunker was more difficult than entering it because the soldiers and looters had haphazardly thrown all sorts of debris on top of the cover of the kessel during their search and ransacking efforts. The extra weight of the rubble made it even more challenging to move the heavy barrel. The son and daughter and my mother worked together to get the opening free, and we all climbed out. It was probably a few hours before daybreak when we emerged. I remember it was still dark outside. My mother picked me up in her arms to carry me, and then she spoke very quietly to me. "Chavale, du vest zayn meine oygn vayl ich ken nit zen (you will be my eyes because I cannot see)," she said. She was night blind. It was the first presentation of her retinitis pigmentosa, a genetic degenerative eye disorder that would progress over Basia's lifetime until she was nearly blind at the end of her life.

We did not know our way around Zhetel and needed the woman and her children to help guide us out of town. But they refused to help. I was still far from healthy and they were concerned that I would be a liability. They were anxious and fearful I would put them at risk. We had gotten to know the character of the family during our time in the bunker. I learned from them that some people are simply more merciful than others, even under trying circumstances.

Bobe Hoda and Mama tried to appeal to the family's conscience, telling them no one knows who is going to live or die. A lot of back and forth and unpleasantness ensued. Basia begged for mercy from the son and the daughter. She was a very proud woman—it was very hard for her to beg. Finally, the children agreed to walk with my mother and me to show us the way out of town, and their mother and Hoda would follow behind a little while after. I imagine our ragged, shoeless quartet of a mother carrying a young child and two twenty-something adults stealing through the darkness was quite a sight. Thankfully, it was August, so our socks sufficed in the warm summer weather.

At the first light of dawn the brother and sister ran away. We were stranded. Worse, there was no sign of my grandmother. "Mir muzn avek fun danent, es drot unzer leben (We have to get out of here, our lives are threatened)," she urged. We started to walk. As we did so, the daylight became a bit stronger and my mother's vision returned. And lo and behold, she spotted my grandmother walking not too far away. She, too, had been abandoned by her erstwhile escort. We were now on our own, walking in unknown territory with no idea where my uncle was or how to find him.

Chaim had made contingency arrangements with Basia in case he could not come back to lead us to the forest himself. We were to get in touch with his contact, a Belorussian farmer named Woska. He was the key to finding Uncle Chaim. My mother knew she would have to search for the farmer with great discretion. She needed to be careful not to inadvertently disclose any details to the wrong person, lest she endanger us, Woska and his family—and Chaim.

In the meantime, Basia and Hoda had also been strategizing their own plan. Their idea was to stop at the home of the gentile to whom Chaim had given all the bolts of our cloth to secure his assistance when the time came. That time was now. Mama left me with Bobe under an overpass a little distance away from the man's home and set off to locate him. She succeeded in finding him, but he told her the timing was not good and she should return in the evening and bring her family. Mama must have been suspicious because she returned to his home earlier than instructed. She had built all her hopes on this man and was crushed when she arrived at his farm and her doubts were confirmed. Mama saw Germans there. But they did not see her. She immediately came to get Bobe and me and we fled.

We had no choice but to walk through open fields now, where we started to see farmers harvesting their crops and shepherds with their flocks. I think the farmers were harvesting corn, as I remember the stalks being very high. We wished each farmer luck with their crops: "Pomaháye Boh," may God help your bounty. As we passed one field we noticed a shepherd looking at us with suspicion, then a similar glance in our direction by another shepherd in the next field. We looked conspicuous, especially in our socks. And we knew that it was just a matter of time before we were betrayed to the Germans. We were right.

We were in an area of dense bush and were hiding in the underbrush when we heard the voices of men shouting and screaming, telling us that they knew where we were and were coming for us. Each of us held her breath. We knew the shepherds must have informed on us. We heard shots and more voices and were sure it would be only minutes until the hunters and their bullets found us.

My bobe wasted no time. "Do is vos mir muzn tohn (Here is what we are going to do)," she said. "Chavale zol zayn der ershter. Du Bashke af Chavale, un ich af dir (will lay down first. You, Bashke, on top of Chavale, and I on top of you)." She added "Ich bin der elster (I am the oldest)." She would sacrifice her life to give my mother and me a chance to survive. I think she could not bear the thought of watching her child and grandchild killed before her eyes. Being the one on top meant she would not have to.

Fortunately, there were no bullets for any of us that day. It was another of the many miracles we experienced during the following years. Somehow, we still believed in them and managed to retain our faith in a Divine spirit willing us to survive. To this day, I do not know how our hunters did not see us because we could see them clearly. We remained silent and still for what felt like an hour before deciding it was safe enough to continue our search for Woska. It was risky, since it was still daylight. But we had no choice. We continued walking, cautiously stopping at farms along the way to ask oblique questions that might bring us to a farm like Woska's without asking directly how to get to it.

We finally found it and warily approached the house. Woska's wife answered the door and told Mama that Woska was not home. I can still picture her, a short woman dressed in traditional peasant garb, with a long wide skirt, a blouse and vest and a small bonnet tied under her chin. It was clear to my mother that the woman was less than happy to see us. She took us around the back of the house, out of sight of the neighbours. I think she may have given us some water but I do not remember actually entering the house.

Woska returned near dusk. His was a far warmer reception, and a tearful one. Woska was a handsome man, with a slightly swarthy complexion and longish dark hair. He was also dressed in typical peasant attire, with baggy pants, a long tunic with a belt tied around his waist and a shirt with cropped sleeves. Woska told us we would leave for the forest right away. It was located on the other side of wetlands at the edge of his property, and we would need to traverse a small river.

This was a daunting prospect for us, as neither my mother, Bobe nor I knew how to swim. But we had no time for trepidation. We departed immediately and got to the crossing point at dusk. Woska pulled out two planks and lay them across the little river. The adults encouraged me to place one wobbly foot in front of the other. "Nokh eyn trot, Chavale. Nokh eyn trot (One more step, Chavale. One more step)," they encouraged as I made my way across the wooden walkway. When we were all safely across, Woska removed the planks and showed us how he carefully hid them.

Woska led us into the forest and directed us to a space between some large pines. He told us to sit down and wait for him. He needed to go back to the farm and get provisions for the rest of our journey. He promised us he would return that evening with food. Before he left, he told my mother the happy news that Rivke and Shael were alive in a nearby forest with a group of survivors from Zhetel. I believe they had escaped from the ghetto after the first liquidation. Woska said he would take us to my aunt and uncle. But first, he had other news to tell us. Terrible news. Heartbreaking news. Chaim was dead. Woska had few details, but shared what he knew. He had heard there had been a dispute with partisans associated with Chaim's unit that resulted in fatalities. Mama was able later to put together the pieces of the story of his death through conversations with other survivors.

Mama and Bobe had suspicions (or maybe knew for sure) that Chaim was already involved with the local partisans when we were still in Lida, which would explain the gun in our apartment that nearly cost Papa his life there. They definitely knew about his activities when we were in Zhetel. Sometime in late 1941, he became an early recruit of a nascent underground of courageous young fighters laying the groundwork for an armed uprising from the ghetto they knew was in the offing. The founder of the group was the leader of Zhetel's Judenrat, a charismatic young lawyer named Alter Dvoretsky.

Alter was a kindred spirit of my uncle. Neither man had any intention of letting the Germans seal our fate unchallenged, and neither had illusions that complying with German rules would change any outcomes. When we were reunited in Zhetel, I remember hearing my wise and prescient uncle tell my mother we should never trust any decrees by the local authorities. They would be lies, used for the purpose of luring us into a false sense of security. He warned Basia and Hoda that the Nazis would be sly and use a variety of ruses, like the scheinen, to methodically subjugate us. Chaim said these coveted little pieces of paper, which so many believed were a passport to safety and survival, were worthless. Their best use was for wiping ourselves after using the toilet.

Chaim's job as a partisan was to help acquire weapons. He went "shopping" among the villagers and farmers in the area, as it was well known they had collected and hidden weapons left behind by Russian soldiers when they retreated after the Germans invaded. Following a successful "buying trip," Chaim would sneak into Zhetel to deliver his purchases and then check on us before slipping back out to repeat the operation. Sometimes he brought precious provisions, such as bread and potatoes from local farms.

The visits became much more difficult once we were in the ghetto. Arousing the suspicions of the Germans was not the only risk. Many Jews in the ghetto believed they would ultimately survive as long as they just followed the rules. Chaim's work was a threat to their sense of security and hope. It is easy to dismiss those fears now but they were wholly understandable for the time. People were afraid of doing anything that might provoke the SS, who would mete out collective punishment.

Even in the face of all the dangers my uncle was undeterred. Chaim knew our future looked grim, but he was at heart an eternal optimist and refused to let us lose hope. I remember hearing him tell Bobe Hoda, "Mama, we are going to win the war, and one day you and I are going to be walking down the streets of Berlin together." This became my own mantra in the forest. I was sure we would win, even though I had no idea then the price of our victory.

In addition to his role as an arms buyer, Chaim liaised with the Soviet partisans in the nearby forest. Alter and his group of Jewish partisans were counting on them to help with the plan to liberate Zhetel's Jews. My uncle was well suited for his job as liaison. He was intelligent, intuitive and amiable. A seasoned partisan, he was familiar with the area, fluent in Russian, a former officer in the Soviet army and a committed communist. I am guessing, based on his daring escape from the POW camp, he was also wily and had nerves of steel.

Unfortunately, despite a common enemy there were frictions within the partisan groups. Jewish partisans were often attacked by non-Jewish partisans, with fatal consequences. Alter and Chaim were two such casualties. Initially we thought the two had been killed together. Alter and several leaders from Zhetel had escaped from the ghetto into the forest on the eve of the first liquidation. Mama had heard that Alter and another man were ambushed and killed on their way back from a meeting with Soviet partisan leadership, and she thought Chaim was the other man.

It was a conclusion based on the limited information we had at the time, but it turned out to be wrong. Basia learned later it was not her brother's body that was found with Alter. Chaim likely died during a partisan mission elsewhere. Military units called *otriads* joined together for big operations. My uncle became part of a consolidation of two otriads, the Orlanski and the Leninski. The Leninski commander was Valentin Botka, a raging anti-Semite. Basia was led to believe that Chaim and his group were betrayed by Botka on a mission to blow up a train.

As with so many of these accounts relayed from survivor to survivor, it is impossible to know for sure exactly what happened to our beloved Chaim. What I do know is that when he returned to us in Lida, my uncle told his mother that he would never again be imprisoned and, further, that he would die with a gun in his hand. The details of his death may not have offered a complete bromide for the pain of his loss, but they did provide a small salve for my wounded heart. I took comfort in knowing that my courageous uncle had left this world as he had hoped. He died on his terms. He died fighting for all of us. He would always be my hero.

There was no time to dwell in grief, no time to mourn. Chaim had done everything he could to help us survive. Now it was up to us to fulfill his plan for our survival, with help from his dear friend Woska. I have no idea how we would have managed without this amazing man. We were totally dependent on him.

Woska returned as promised that same night, bringing with him potatoes, onions, carrots and crispy pieces of fried lard called *skwarski*. We made a feast of everything except the skwarski. Ironically, it was that food which made me long desperately for Uncle Chaim.

It reminded me of how he would "hide" his lard from my Bobe Hoda in Zhetel.

After we were fortified, Woska led us deeper into the woods to where Rivke and Shael were hiding with a group of other survivors. It was dusk when we left Woska's farm and light when we arrived at our destination. I imagine this incredible man would have been more content to deliver us safely into the hands of his friend Chaim. But that was not to be. I can only guess at the strength of their bond for Woska to put his life and his family at risk for us. Woska saw us into the forest as promised, and the time came to say goodbye. It was an emotional farewell. There would never be enough words of gratitude for what he had done, never enough words for three lives saved.

The reunion with my aunt and uncle was bittersweet—joy that we were all together once again and sadness for the loss of Chaim. In addition, what should have counted as happy news did not. My aunt was pregnant. I know how much my mother loved her sister, but I have no doubt that Rivke's pregnancy fed the growing weight of Mama's anxieties and stress. She was visibly upset. She felt that her sister had been careless at a time when she should have been extra cautious. However, any recriminations or reprimands would have to wait. We needed to move. Death was chasing us. Perhaps it would not find us in the depths of the forest.

The Forest

August 1942 – September 1944

The forest Waska led us into, was called Ludzichy.

It was near a village of the same name, about ten kilometres west and slightly south of Zhetel. The woods were part of Puszcza Lipiczańska, the Lipichanska Forest, an extensive woodland network that had become a refuge for thousands of survivors from ghettos, shtetls and concentration camps in the area. It was also the base for many Jewish and Soviet partisan units, including Chaim's.

As my family and I walked farther into the puszcza, I was struck by a sense of awe and wonder. The ancient forest was so foreign to me. The density of the old-growth oak and pine trees was so thick we could barely see the sky. I remember the size of the trees was daunting and gave me a sense of foreboding. I felt very small. Yet, at the same time, the untamed environment was also inviting. After being in the ghetto, the forest felt like a haven. Over time, I became acclimated to my new wilderness home, and it felt like a sanctuary. It was in the puszcza that I developed a love for birds. Perhaps it was the sweet innocence of their song that moved me. When I saw the trees being born in the spring, I felt like I was benefitting from their rebirth, the young leaves on the branches renewing my sense of hope. When things were peaceful in the puszcza, it was a heavenly atmosphere. I felt safe there. I felt that God was closer in the forest than in the city.

We entered the forest in mid-summer, when the weather was mild and the trees were lush and full. We were still wearing the thick woollen socks that we had donned before we left the ghetto, and fortunately for us, the forest floor beneath our feet was still soft and dry. It would be a whole different story once the seasons changed.

I wonder if Woska briefed Basia and Hoda about life in the forest as we walked from his farm into the forest. Perhaps he imparted some basic survival tips to them. Even if yes, how much could he have prepared them in such a short time together? Chaim was supposed to tutor us in puczcza life—maybe he had started to do that on his visits with us in Zhetel. But he was gone, unable to help us now or answer our myriad questions. It would be up to the other partisans in the forests to educate us. We would learn from them and from the members of the family groups who had already established themselves in the wilds, especially those from other nearby towns who were familiar with the area.

We became part of a small *semejnaja gruppa*, Russian for "family group." These groups were made up of relatives of partisans and non-relatives. Non-combatants, they came together for mutual support, pooling resources for food and shelter, forming little communal camps composed of a few families to hundreds of people.

My family group was never large, perhaps a dozen of us at most. Rivke and Shael were not always with us. Sometimes they would leave, likely to be with people Shael knew from Zhetel. Like most family groups, ours ebbed and flowed as new members joined, left or were killed. Each time a new survivor joined or passed through, it was like a celebration—joy and tears and anxious questions. "Did you see so-and-so? Do you remember my so-and-so? What happened to you?"

For a time, in addition to my mother and grandmother, my little group included Motl Bielski's widow, Malka, and their sons, Yisroel and Yosef. The family now included Malka's "forest husband," Yitzhak Rubenstein. This kind, gentle widower reminded me of my father, and I reminded him of his daughter who had been killed. I think he was from Novogrudek. He shared extra scraps of food with me, always giving me more than he kept for himself. He was a rare human being. At some point, he, Malka, Yisroel and Yosef moved to a different part of the forest. Yitzhak and Malka were legally married after the war.

The partisans did their best to help shield the family groups from harm. However, this was somewhat challenging since the merest whisper of a threat sent us on the move. And the whispers were frequent. We were rarely in one place long enough to develop total dependence on the partisans. We had to become as self-sufficient as possible.

We had learned the rules of the ghetto and we had survived. Now we would have to learn the rules of the forest. And we would have to learn them very, very well and very, very quickly. We could either adapt and hopefully live or not adapt and definitely die. Small mistakes could cost not only our lives but also the lives of those in our immediate group and of others hiding nearby. We became fanatical about the three golden rules of the forest: 1) Always be vigilant; 2) Never stay in one place for too long; and 3) Never get complacent.

These were the critical pillars of our "torah" of forest survival. The rest, as the great sage Rabbi Hillel might have advised, was commentary. It was up to us to go forth and learn it. And that is exactly what we did.

Life in the forest was harsh and unrelentingly challenging. Those who survived were skilled at blending into the environment. They could sense danger from miles away. They were relentlessly vigilant, clever, swift and bold. They were also lucky.

The trials of living rough were manifested in the myriad tasks of life in the woods. Women took over the tasks that normally fell to men, as there were few in the family groups. Many men had joined the partisans. My mother, Basia, had no time for deliberating gender roles. She did the same chores as the men: chopping wood, building fires, hunting for food. Basia did whatever needed to be done.

Nothing was too difficult for her. She attacked all her tasks with stoicism and resolve. Her job was keeping our family alive. And she never had a day off.

In addition to the physical challenges there were also the unrelenting psychological ones. There was never a time when we could let down our guard. We lived with the constant nervous anticipation of being discovered and killed at any moment. We were careful to speak quietly. We were always alert. We became as hypersensitized and wary as the creatures of the forest. The wildlife were our survival barometers. We observed their every movement. We were as watchful as owls and as responsive as deer. We monitored the birds and rabbits. When the wildlife became agitated, so did we. When they were at ease, so were we. The smallest sound, the merest twitch of a twig or even a leaf that fell to the ground might all be harbingers of danger. I remember after the war seeing the movie *Bambi* and feeling a strong connection with that young fawn.

Remarkably, I never feared dying in the woods. Or at least it is not part of my conscious memory from that time. However, I do remember feeling the same fear in the forest—of being captured alive—as I had in the ghetto. And tortured. It is not hard to understand why I was obsessed with these thoughts. Try as the adults might to shield me from their discussions, I had big ears. And they were impossible to shut. It was difficult not to listen when the adults spoke. When they discussed the news, I heard. And when they spoke of stories of survivors who had escaped from the ghetto to the forest only to be caught there and tortured before death, I heard those, too. My only thought and prayer was that, if I were going to die, it would be a quick death. During those times I always thought of my friend Svetlana, from Lida. When she fled the city, her father gave her mother a gun and told her, "If you encounter the enemy, remember, you shoot the children first and then yourself." It made an indelible imprint on my mind.

My recollection of our time in the forest is of always being on the run—or, at least, of not remaining very long in one place. Maybe we stayed put for a few months. But that was a long stretch. We relied on the intel and counsel of the partisans and other Jews we encountered in the forest to help feed us information. We moved when they told us. During respites of flight, we sought temporary shelter between the trees. We slept on the ground under lean-tos or little hut-like shelters we made from the branches of young trees and pieces of wood and camouflaged as best we could.

In cooler weather we lay on the forest floor like sardines in a can, one body tucked up next to the other to conserve body heat. In winter, when temperatures dropped too low to sleep on the ground, we built a crude dugout in the ground called a *zemlyanka*, Russian for "earth house." It provided protection against the elements and concealed us from the unrelenting threat of two-legged hunters. And there were far too many of those.

The Germans had plenty of eager volunteers—local villagers and collaborators—who knew the terrain far better than they did. Their zealous helpers acted as the Nazis' advance guard. Already steeped in nationalism and anti-Semitism, they were further incited by German propaganda that portrayed Jews as Christ killers and enemies of the state. The collaborators rooted us out, informed the Nazis of our whereabouts and collected their rewards: some salt, sugar, eggs, alcohol or small sums of money. They were especially adept at making us easy targets, by setting up blockades in the forest, hemming us in and cutting off escape routes. They hunted us like animals, often using dogs to track us down.

I remember living in two *zemlyanki* during our time in the forest, one for each winter that we were in hiding. Building a zemlyanka was labour intensive and time consuming. Mama was responsible for building ours. Everyone in the group pitched in, sharing whatever tools they had to hand—perhaps a knife or a small shovel taken from farmers during a foray for food and supplies, or borrowed from partisans. Although such chores were a group effort, not every male took to them with alacrity. I can still see Mama, with her ulcerated leg, working like a lumberjack to cut the young trees with a borrowed saw and using her hands to strip the branches for the wood to reinforce the walls of the dugout and make the roof. It took her several days of work to complete our zemlyanka.

They were as basic as basic could be, with none of the furnishings or accessories, like tarps, bunks or even cooking stoves that I sometimes heard about in other family and partisan camps. Our first zemlyanka was maybe five square feet for six of us. The second one was larger, around ten square feet for seven of us. Each was deep enough that the adults could just clear the roof when they sat up straight. There was room enough for a little fire, which we were very careful to light only when we felt the risk of the smoke betraying our hiding spot was low.

Needless to say, hygiene and maintaining our health in the forest was hugely challenging. We were malnourished and vitamin deficient. We were unwashed and unkempt. We wore the same clothes day after day with no relief. We were filthy skeletons, bulked up only by the layers of our lice-infested clothing, which were wore twenty-four hours a day. I often wonder how we managed to survive those two years without bathing. We lived in very close quarters, especially inside our zemlyanki, which did not help the situation. Our communal life meant we shared everything, including germs and vermin. We were textbook breeding grounds for both. Bacteria loved us. Lice adored us. We were constantly covered in a host of skin rashes. Frostbite in the winter claimed fingers and toes. Gums bled from pyorrhea. And many women, including my mother, lost their menstrual cycle during this period, an ironic godsend.

Illustration based on Evelyn's recollection of her family's Zemlyanka in the forest.

A potato sack did double-duty as a giant plate. I cannot remember eating utensils. We used our hands and drank soup out of a small pot. I do remember we had a metal pail for collecting water from rain or fresh water streams and springs.

We used axle grease when we could get it to treat the big pustules of the uncomfortable boils on our bodies and our scalps and on our faces, near our eyes. The grease was slippery and black, and it smelled terrible. When the boils were cured, they left huge marks on the skin. I was covered with them. One mark on my knee lasted several years before it finally disappeared. We also suffered from scabies between our fingers, which we treated when we could with a thick yellow ointment that had a strong smell of sulphur. I do not know why, but Mama and Bobe were thankfully never plagued by either boils or scabies.

Our suffering was chronic. But never once do I remember hearing anyone in our group complain about the one hardship suffered by all: hunger. The elders did not say anything, so neither did I. In truth, I am not even sure how to explain what it felt like, perhaps because there came a point when we just learned to ignore the gnawing emptiness in our bellies. Days could go by when we had nothing, especially when it was too dangerous to go begging because the enemy was too close. Going hungry was the norm. Getting fed was an occasion, and the occasions became fewer and farther between.

The acquisition of food was a constant challenge and the responsibility for gathering it was left up to the members of the family groups. In our case, that duty fell to my mother. She did not go out every day, especially in the winter, when she would trudge—in temperatures reaching -40°C—through snow up to her thighs across the frozen marshes and lakes with a small scouting party to beg or steal provisions from local farmers. For two years Basia balanced the risk of our starvation with the risk of losing her life. It is true that many (most) farmers were unfeeling or, worse, informers. But it is important to acknowledge that there were those who hung onto their humanity during the war, righteous gentiles who were sympathetic and compassionate and gave us food and other necessities. People like Woska.

On a successful trip Mama might return with a burlap potato sack, barely filled with some onions, a bit of cheese, a few eggs, some milk and a little bread. Potatoes in winter were a real treat. I remember roasting them in the ashes of a small fire outdoors or in our zemlyanka. I can still taste them. So good—no butter, no salt, just plain. In summertime, we collected tiny wild forest strawberries called *poziomki* to add to our meagre sustenance. I remember gathering them in the hem of my dress to bring back and save for later, but often it was more of an eat-as-you-go operation. I just plucked the little red gems from the bushes and popped them immediately into my mouth, where they burst with the most delightful sweetness. Those strawberries felt like a gift from God. They reminded me of my prewar life, when I could enjoy this kind of simple summer pleasure without fear of death. It felt long ago and far away.

The Puszcza

Polish for "primeval forest" or "ancient woodland," a *puszcza* refers to an expansive, largely untouched natural landscape. Dense and ecologically varied, *puszcze* (plural form) are interlaced with rivers, bogs and open meadows supporting a wide variety of wildlife. Western Belarus is home to a vast network of such puszcze, forming an extensive ecological complex that stretches across thousands of square kilometres. Many are named after nearby towns and villages, while others incorporate the word puszcza in their names—such as Puszcza Lipiczańska and Puszcza Naliboki.

Not every foray ended in success. We were careful to conserve whatever food Basia managed to bring back. Also critical were non-edible provisions. When she went scrounging she would ask if a farmer had anything for a child. It didn't matter if it was too big. If she were lucky, Mama returned from one of her trips with a warm coat or other piece of clothing. One time she brought back a man's sheepskin jacket, which served as a coat for me. Another time she came home with a blanket. There were few blankets in the forest and every one was dear. She stuffed too-large shoes with leaves to take up space. My feet were always protected—unlike hers.

Mama spared nothing for herself. She spent our entire time in the forest without shoes. All she had were foot coverings she made for herself by wrapping burlap potato sacks and rags over the now-tattered woollen socks she had worn out of the Zhetel ghetto. I cannot fathom how she managed, especially in the winter. I often wish I had asked her more questions after the war about this time. But by then we were all focused on the future and did not want to dwell on the past.

As strong as Mama was and as young as I was, I remember one particular occasion when our roles were reversed. It happened during an *oblava*, Russian for "manhunt" or "raid."

An oblava usually happened in the very early dawn, when we were not yet fully roused and thus at our most vulnerable. Vigilance was always the watchword in the forest. Adults took turns being on guard duty, and everyone was always very careful and conscious of his or her surroundings, just like animals are. By now we had developed a sixth sense to note the smallest disruptions in the sounds of the forest. But the old-timers had the most sensitive antennae. Often, it was they who sensed first when an ambush was imminent. Sometimes before the lookouts could alert everyone, the old-timers shouted, "Oblava! Oblava!," giving us a few precious moments to scatter and flee to safety. And if there were a spare second or two, there might be time to bury a utensil or other item under some leaves or in the hollow of a nearby tree. Speed was the key to survival, so my mother would grab me and together with my grandmother we would race away.

It is impossible to truly convey in words what these ambushes were like in terms of sheer terror: the panic that spurs you in seconds from sleep to your feet and in motion, away from the hunters—shooting and shouting as they bay for your blood; deciding in split seconds which way to turn—which direction is life and which, death; the heart-pounding fear of crashing through the trees, trying not to trip on an exposed tree root, or forcing your freezing limbs through deep snow, frantically looking for somewhere—anywhere—to conceal yourself, hoping, praying that yours will not be the body felled by a bullet and left on the forest floor; or worse, my own greatest fear, caught like a contagion from the adults, of being captured alive and tortured before being put to death.[1]

Oblavas could go on for hours. We would run toward an area of dense trees where we could hide behind their trunks. This was easier in spring, summer and early fall. Winter was more treacherous. We would just run as far ahead of the hunters as we could. We stopped when we no longer heard gunshots. Then we waited. When it had been quiet for a long time, we would emerge tentatively from wherever we had hidden and try to retrace our steps to find our way back to where we had started—and meet up with the other survivors. It was tortuous. We would find bodies, marking them in our minds so they could be retrieved for burial, if possible. When we were lucky, our hunters—running in a frenzy of bloodthirst—bypassed our makeshift "campsite," and some small article might still be where we left it—a blanket, a fallen shoe or a buried "treasure." Otherwise, we returned to find our belongings trashed or stolen, forcing us to start again, begging anew from the farmers and relying on the partisans to help replenish what we lost.

I remember a rare occasion when I was the one who took the lead in guiding us back. My mother had run with me during an oblava and had become disoriented. She turned to me. "Chavale, vu zoln mir geyn, rechts oder links (which way should we go, right or left)?" I thought about it for a few seconds and then gave her my answer. Fortunately, my choice was correct and we found our way back to the right spot. It still amazes me that after running in a blind panic, with no pre-planned route, we managed to find our way "home." It was as though we developed tracking and visual mapping skills in the forest. Landscapes imprinted themselves upon us, and we just knew our way back. Forty years after this oblava I asked my mother why she had asked me to guide us, and why she had felt she could rely on my answer. Mama responded that the reservoir of her own intuition was empty at that point and she needed mine. She added that she had a

1 In 1982, I was on a land tour that included a fox hunt. When the dogs were let loose to take up the scent of the fox, I felt like I was back in the forest. I was the fox and the hunters were the Nazis and their collaborators. At the end of the hunt, we were served sherry in crystal glasses to celebrate the success of the kill. To toast death. It was the same ritual that took place during the Holocaust when the Nazis would get drunk on schnapps to celebrate their own victorious kills.

sense that somehow my innocence and the purity of my child's soul would engender the right answer.

There were countless hazards in the forest and the dangers were unending. Yet, even with all our hardships we felt blessed to have the freedom of the open spaces and fortunate that we were not in a concentration camp. Many of us even managed not to lose faith that we would survive.

Bobe Hoda shared my optimism that we would walk out of the forest one day. And I know Chaim had hope until the day he died. My own faith is something that still amazes me more than nearly eight decades on. It was a lasting gift from my father, who nurtured it in me since early childhood. Even throughout the darkest times of the Holocaust and my life, I always felt I could count on God for help, that He would not abandon me. I never saw God as a vengeful being. Rather, my understanding was always of a benevolent, loving and compassionate source for all humankind, because we are all His children, each one created in His image.

That faith and optimism never waned in me during our time in the forest, even when our luck seemed about to run out. Two particular occasions spring to mind. One occurred in the winter of 1942–43. We were tucked inside our small zemlyanka, which we had taken pains to carefully camouflage with tree branches. That morning I could see some watery light filtering through them. We were lying down, crowded together inside the confined space of the bunker, when we heard the sounds of branches snapping outside. We knew by now the different sounds that animals made as they moved through the woods. Boots crunching on the snow confirmed our worst fears. The sound made us all stiffen. I was enough of a veteran by then to know that I must remain quiet and still. I do not remember how long it was that we sat holding our collective breath until the footsteps faded away. When the light had completely faded to dark, we crawled out of our zemlyanka and fled to a new part of the forest. Logically, I understood we were in danger of being discovered. But as we sat listening and waiting for the footsteps of our hunters to recede, I never wavered in my belief that they would not find us.

The second event happened the following summer. We were milling about when we heard shooting very nearby. Our hunters were already close enough that I could hear them shouting, "It's just a matter of time before we get you." People started to run in different directions. It was complete chaos and I somehow got separated from my family. I had no idea where I was running. I just remember a woman running behind me was felled by a bullet. By some miracle, my mother found me and my family was reunited. I do not use this word "miracle" lightly. Mama told me that many others had not been as fortunate as us, and members of our family group had been killed. It was frightening. The bullet that had killed the woman behind me could have easily killed me. It took us a long time to recover from that massacre. And to bury the dead.

The partisan battalions in our region used to move between the Lipichanska and Naliboki Forests. Family groups like ours, especially those who had relatives in the partisans, did our best to try and stay as close to the fighters as possible, both for safety and sustenance. The Jewish partisans sometimes came by. My grandmother and mother developed a casual acquaintance with them in the forest, and they shared with us some of their supplies, as well as food and other necessities they had confiscated during raids. A small pot, a knife or some flint or matches for lighting fires were especially precious gifts. They also filled us in on the latest news of the war. When it was deemed safe enough, a few partisans even remained to visit for a few hours with our little group. We were careful always to speak in whispered voices.

These wonderful men even brought me precious gifts on a few occasions. One time it was a pair of shoes, another time an outfit made out of a parachute. I especially loved the rare occasion when a few partisans joined us in our zemlyanka. We lit a fire and sang, accompanied by one of the partisans on his *garmon*, a small Russian accordion—at a low volume—while watchers remained vigilant outside. The partisans took popular songs from Moscow and changed them into patriotic, emotional songs, rich melodies with soulful lyrics about life and loss. Original Russian tunes were also translated into Hebrew, with lyrics reflecting the common fight for freedom. I picked up the new songs quickly. I can only remember singing in the zemlyanka twice, but I treasured those special times. For those brief hours, my life was normal. I could be for a while just a little girl who liked to sing.

Two songs stand out in my mind. "Tyomnaya Noch" was a famous song written by a Russian composer for a 1943 war film called *Two Soldiers.* In it, a soldier on a dark night in a dugout on the Russian front sings of his longing for his wife and baby at home. It was translated into Hebrew with the title "Efel Laylah." The other song was "Na opuške lesa," about a comrade who falls in battle at the edge of the forest and the friend who witnesses his death. It, too, was translated into Hebrew and reworked as "b'Aravot Hanegev," a well-known song of Israel's 1948 War of Independence.

Singing with the partisans was a chance to temporarily slip away from the realities of our lives. But those respites were few and far between, so we did our best to improvise other fun pastimes. And boy, were we creative! One of our favourite diversions involved lice.

We turned the scourge of these typhus-causing parasites into both a game and an educational opportunity. "Lice Lessons: Itchucation" was a fun interdisciplinary hands-on unit in the natural sciences curriculum of zemlyanka "home school." It was suitable for students of all ages—everyone could play and everyone could learn. Best of all, we never had to worry about running out of supplies. Our resources were infinite! Had there been an award given for the "Most Lice in a Zemlyanka," we would have won first place.

The lesson began with the "Bonfire of the Lice." We would shake our clothes over a fire and watch as the parasites dropped into the flames and burned. The ones that stubbornly remained on our bodies became specimens for study, the special forte of our autodidact resident lice expert, Yosef. He was a member of our forest family and shared our zemlyanki with us both winters. Yosef's nickname was Shpronjernover, the spring coil. The moniker suited him perfectly. He was wiry and tense, with a lot of nervous energy. Yosef survived the forest, but not the war. I believe he died in the Soviet army.

Yosef was a lice master. He would carefully take a specimen and examine it over the light of the fire. Then, after careful consideration, he would decide how to classify it. He took his work and pedagogy very seriously. He was fascinated by the vermin. And like a true entomologist, Yosef even created categories and hierarchies for them. It was hard not to be impressed with Yosef's powers of observation. He discovered that we hosted at least seven varieties of lice.

These included black, yellow, green and albino lice, all with distinctive sizes, shapes, legs and heads.

After Yosef had finished identifying and classifying each specimen, the vermin was doomed. Again, Yosef used his natural teaching ability to help us hone our technique on how to kill the pests. Our weapons were our thumbs or, more specifically, our thumbnails. Yosef showed us how to make a "lice sandwich" by trapping a louse between our thumbnails and quickly pressing the nails tightly together at a bit of an angle to one another so they fit snugly together without any space between them. We then gave a subtle little twist of the united nails, crushing the little bloodsucker and taking great satisfaction in watching the parasite, swollen with our blood, explode. The gifted among us could crush several lice at a time in this manner.

In addition to providing endless diversion and teachable moments, lice also provided a great topic of conversation. It was impossible to have a social exchange with strangers or friends in the forest without swapping lice stories. Other than those lighthearted exchanges, though, I remember very little silly talk. Conversations were about survival and a future world where we lived in peace and harmony. Where we could relish the mundane chores of everyday life, and where parents could nurture their children with joy instead of fear. We were so confident that some of us would survive and do all of these things. We just had no idea who those survivors would be.

In the winter of 1943, our survival and that of the members of our group became complicated. When we had reunited with Rivke and Shael the previous summer, my aunt must have been about four months pregnant. She had barely a hint of a baby bump then. Even at full term, she barely showed. Deprivation and starvation will do that. I imagine, though, that her pregnancy must have been a source of stress for her. I know it was for Hoda and Basia. Ensuring the safe delivery of a baby would push everyone's stress to new heights.

Rivke's contractions began on January 30. The snow was knee-deep and the temperature well below zero. We were not in a zemlyanka because there had been an oblava, one of the rare times I remember our hunters braving sub-zero temperatures to hunt us. We had been chased for a long time and when we finally stopped running, there was no opportunity to build a shelter before Rivke began feeling contractions. To make matters more complicated I was sick with a high fever, chills and a rash all over my body. I was suffering from typhus. Given that I was infested with lice, it is a miracle I had not caught it until then. There was no medicine in the forest, no antibiotics, no doctor. There was just my mother and her inherent wisdom. Again, as she had in Zhetel when I had scarlet fever, my mother nursed me back to health. She melted snow on a small fire so I would have something warm to drink and keep hydrated. I remember that she also cut my hair short in an effort to rid me of head lice.

Rivke laboured through the day, and Basia and Hoda began to worry that my aunt would need help delivering the baby. They knew of a young midwife named Rochel, who was in a forest near Nakrishok, about seven or eight kilometres from where we were. The decision was made to find Rochel and bring her back. Rivke's husband, Shael, was designated to get her, but he refused. It was not until Basia told him she would go with him that he relented, and the two set out for Nakrishok

While my mother and Shael were away, members of our group dug into the ice-covered earth to create a birthing pit for my aunt and layered it with warm clothing. The pit was not that deep, maybe a few feet, but freezing swamp water began to seep into it. The men did their best to assist the women, using a bucket and their hands to bail the water. I think they bailed forty buckets, but the water kept pooling back into the pit. Rivke laboured for hours without a sound, while all of us silently prayed there would not be another oblava in the middle of the baby's delivery. Hoda helped her daughter walk around, and when Rivke could no longer walk she sat in the pit. In the beginning she bit down on her finger when a wave of pain washed over her. Hoda supported her head and later gave Rivke a small piece of wood to place between her teeth as Rivke's labour progressed and the contractions grew stronger.

Around midnight, Shael and my mother returned with Rochel, well in time for the delivery. Given all the challenges of their trip, it is incredible they made it at all. They could not travel in the open or take a road (even if there were one). They had to proceed stealthily and cautiously through the forest, weaving their way in the dark of night through the trees, in the freezing cold and through deep snow, all the while wondering if the raiders who had been at our heels earlier were gone or still on the hunt. They had to find the camp where Rochel was, convince her to come with them and then do the whole trip in reverse. It is a mystery to me to this day how they managed it. How did they navigate their way in the dark? How did they even know how and where to find Rochel? What motivated that incredible woman to come with my mother and risk her own life to bring forth new life? Children were dying in the forest, not being born.

After Rivke's son was safely delivered and Shael left to accompany Rochel back to her camp, the rest of our group told Hoda that her grandson should be suffocated. My grandmother stood firm against them. "Der kind vet leben (This child shall live)!" she declared with conviction. "We are going to name him Yosef, after his grandfather. You need not worry. He will be in my care. I will be running with him during all the oblavas. And I will not be running with you. I will be running against you."

Up until my cousin was born, Bobe Hoda slept next to me in the zemlyanka. After my aunt gave birth, Bobe moved and slept next to Rivke and the baby. A man in our zemlyanka named Ruvke eagerly took my bobe's former place next to me and I remember him rubbing up against me. I told my mother about it and she switched places to sleep next to this pervert. He did not survive the war. Although I disliked him very much, I still felt a lot of guilt about his death.

For the rest of our time in the forest, my grandmother devoted herself to keeping her grandson alive. His mother nursed him but she was so malnourished there was little to give her son, and his circumcision (traditionally done on the eighth day after birth) was out of the question in the forest. (Joseph was not circumcised until age three, after the war). Bobe Hoda basically glued herself to Rivke and Joseph, walking with them in case she needed to grab the baby and run with him. Any time there was an oblava Hoda stuck her thumb in Joe's mouth to prevent him from crying. She would then dash with him in a different direction from where the rest of our group was headed in order to increase everyone's chances of survival.

Joseph learned the basic skills of crawling and walking on the rough forest floor. When he saw a birch tree, he hugged it as a beloved friend. When he saw a fir tree, he closed his eyes and ran away from it.

I never knew why the different species elicited these opposite responses. He started walking at around nine months and as far as I was concerned he was hands down the cutest creature in the forest. He was blond haired and blue eyed, like his mother. He was confident in his surroundings and instinctively knew when to stay quiet. He wore a blue cotton tunic my grandmother made for him I think out of a parachute given to us by a partisan. I have no idea how she managed to make it blue. Maybe it was blue to start.

In February 1943, shortly after Joseph's birth, we moved to a different forest within the Lipichanska Forest. I believe it had to do with the Nazis ramping up their efforts to hunt down the partisans who were escaping farther into the puszcze of Western Belarus. The fighters were completing more and more missions, and the Germans were devoting more and more resources to finding and killing them. The deeper the partisans went, the deeper we refugees were also forced to go to elude the hunters.

Beyond knowing that we never left the Lipichanska Forest, I do not remember the name of the new forest where we took refuge that winter. All I know is that there was no discernable difference between where we moved to and where we had been. As far as I could tell, our new location was interchangeable with the old one. It looked the same, felt the same. It was all the same. Deprivation. Fear. Hunger. Oblavas. Fleeing. Uncertainty. Lice. Nothing had changed.

And for the next eighteen months, nothing would.

PART THREE
Refugees

Liberation

September 1944 – June 1945

During the summer of 1944, the partisans informed us liberation was near.

They told us the Soviets were about to liberate the oppressed of Eastern Europe, which was, of course, music to our ears. However, they admonished us to still be careful and remain cautious; the Germans were fleeing into the forests and the situation was still dangerous. I wondered how those "invincible" master-race Germans felt to be running scared now. The hunters were now the hunted. The tide of the war had finally turned in our favour. The real march of the living was about to begin and soon the *churban*, the destruction of the Jewish people, would be revealed to the world. It was then that my mother found the courage to tell me that my father was dead. I could have filled an ocean with the tears I shed then, tears I had been holding at bay for a very long time.

Jews in the Forest

The exact number of Jews who sought refuge in the forests of Eastern Europe remains unknown. There are no lists, only scholarly estimates. Israeli historian Yehuda Bauer estimated that twenty to thirty thousand Jewish partisans and civilians lived in the woodland sanctuaries of Eastern Europe, and only about one-third to one-half of those walked out after liberation.

In early September, Yosef the lice expert asked me to go with him for a walk to a nearby stream. Along the way, he said he could hear Russian being spoken in the distance. We moved a little closer to the source of the sound, careful to stay hidden. Peeking through the widely-spaced narrow-trunked young trees, we spotted two soldiers standing on a nearby road. We inched even closer, straining to identify if they were friends or foes. I could feel Yosef's tension. He thought the men might be collaborators, and we primed ourselves to run. But then I noticed their uniforms. I had seen the same ones on the soldiers in Lida. These were Soviets. I was further reassured when I saw their *kuchnya*, a portable kitchen with a tall chimney. That was also a familiar sight. I remembered these Soviet army cooking trailers from Eishyshok. Yosef's tension ebbed. We decided to take a chance and approach the men.

WWII Soviet army kuchnya (mobile military field kitchen), c. 1940s.

The soldiers were definitely not collaborators. We got closer, and a big Russian grabbed me and hugged me. "Doragaya dochka (Darling daughter)," he said with deep emotion. And then they started to cry. I reminded them of the daughters they had left behind. Each of us was so overjoyed to see the other. They were warm and kind and obviously loved children. We took the men back to where our group was gathered and everyone just stared at them with a mix of fear and relief. It was the first time we had seen Soviet soldiers during our time in the forest. "We are here, you are liberated," they said. "But be very, very careful. The Germans and their accomplices are on the run. And they are heading to the forest. You must leave here as soon as possible," they cautioned.

The date was September 7, 1944. We must have been very close to Zhetel at that point, as it did not take us—and the other groups nearby—very long to walk with our liberators and the other soldiers into town, all the while singing Russian songs. It all felt very strange. I was supposed to be overjoyed. And I was. We all were. But at the same time, I felt a deep sense of loss. The forest had become my home. My town. My community. I turned to my mother. "Mama, lomir geyn tsurik in vald (Let's go back)," I told her. I had encountered so much bloodshed in Zhetel, I could not imagine it ever returning to normal.

Word spread quickly, and many more survivors came out of hiding. Of the roughly six hundred Jews from Zhetel who fled to the forest, only two hundred survived. Of those who did walk out alive that September day, only a tiny fraction were child survivors like myself. From our extended group in the woods, there were few children besides Yosef and Yisroel Bielski, my cousin and me. We had no way of knowing it then, but my family would be one of only two from Eishyshok to survive the Holocaust with members of three generations.

The wounded and those too weak to walk were transported on army trucks. Rivke carried Joseph, now aged eighteen months, in her arms. Poor little Joseph, the drastic change of scenery and the sight of the houses was so frightening that he began to scream. The little boy who had run through the forest, petting the leaves on the trees and shying away from the ones with thorns could not be put down. It took Rivke a very long time to console him. He became very clingy and needed to be held constantly for a long time after that.

One of the soldiers who accompanied us into town was a handsome, young Jewish doctor. He confided to the adults that we should not linger in Zhetel. There was a lot of anti-Semitism in the Soviet army, and we should head west as soon as we could. He also patiently explained to us how to treat our boils, telling us we needed to eat fat. So, we started to eat butter and anything we could get from the farmers that was rich in fat. Unfortunately for little Joseph, the rich foods gave him dysentery and he became very ill. Thankfully, the doctor successfully treated him.

My family returned to the Zhetel home of Shael Joselewitz's family. To my child's eyes, the house seemed very spacious. Only Shael's brothers, Yechiel and Ephraim, lived in it. When we got there, we were taken immediately to the back of the house. A little area was set up for us where we could strip out of our clothes, which were summarily taken and burned. I remember standing in the nude and having my hair rinsed with kerosene. The smell made me nauseous, but it was worth it to get rid of the lice. I think our replacement clothes came from friends of the Joselewitzes, and from townspeople in Zhetel. Food, too; people brought eggs, and I have a particular memory of a large globe of butter covered with a thick cheesecloth to keep it moist.

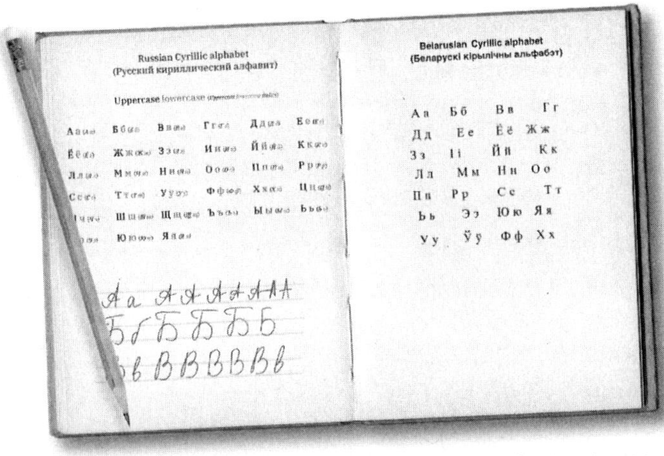

Example of Soviet elementary school primer used in Zhetel, 1944.

I believe we remained in Zhetel for around three months. During that time, I began classes at a local school, along with other child survivors from the forest. I was one of the youngest. I started studying the Russian and Ukrainian alphabets simultaneously, which was very confusing. Less confusing were my feelings for my first crush. The object of my affection was a handsome Russian boy named Grisha. He had wavy blond hair and blue eyes, and he was very bright. His father was a teacher at my school and also held some sort of position of prominence in town. I remember bringing his family matzoh at Passover and them being very appreciative of my gift.

Grisha and I were chosen as representatives from our school to take a wreath to the *tserkva*, the Russian Orthodox church, for the funeral service of Mikhail, a student a few years younger than us. The interior of the church was dark and gloomy but very opulent with a lot of icons and ornamentation. I remember the scent of the heavy incense made me feel faint. However, I did appreciate the music of the liturgy and the beautiful voices of the clergy leading the services. Grisha and I approached the front of the church to lay our wreath near where

Example of Pionieri uniform, and Lenin pin, c. 1944.

Mikhail rested serenely in an open coffin. I remember he was dressed in white silk. I was both awed and impressed by the scene before me.

In addition to going to school, I was inducted into the Young Pioneers, the Pionieri, a Soviet youth organization similar to Scouts, but broader (and agenda driven). Although membership was hypothetically voluntary, social pressure ensured that almost every child between the ages of nine and fifteen joined the movement.

The group promoted communist ideology through life skills, sports, games, camp and the like. Our group leader was a young Jewish girl. She taught us all about the glorious Soviet leaders—Lenin, Marx and Stalin—whose portraits were ubiquitous throughout our school and classrooms. We were introduced to Russian culture, learned the new national anthem, and became very fervent and dedicated to our mission to become good little communists. We were given red scarves to wear around our necks with a special pin. I wore mine with great pride. I remember the Pionieri slogans were Matushka Rossiya, Mother Russia, and Stalin Otyetz, Father Stalin.

In keeping with the Russians' love for its rich arts culture, the Pionieri also encouraged music and dance. They selected the most talented children for performances. A classmate, a survivor from the forest named Keren, and I were selected to learn the hopak, a Ukrainian folk dance that evolved from an all-male celebratory dance by Cossacks to include male and female dancers. I was assigned the male role as I was the stronger dancer. We performed the dance together at a regional competition in a theatre and won first prize!

Shortly after our dance competition our group leader told Keren and me that we had much "merit" and should go to Moscow to study and further our talent in folk dancing. On one hand, we were very excited. But on the other hand, we feared the idea of separating from our families to go to Moscow. Thankfully, neither of our families pursued the idea.

My family was also not keen on staying in Zhetel any longer than necessary. Mama, Bobe and Rivke were fervent capitalists, and the prospect of being Soviet citizens held no appeal. As for me, maybe there was a touch of Uncle Chaim in me after all. I found my new life in Zhetel very appealing. All I could see were positives—all the support I was getting, all the interest in me such as from Merele, my dance teacher, who recognized I was an innate performer. I felt very at home on the stage now and did not want to think about leaving. Maybe I would become a professional dancer?

I could not for the life of me figure out what we were running away from. What was not to like? I was too young and naïve to understand that I was being indoctrinated, though Mama had no concerns about me becoming a Marxist-Leninist. She was just happy that I was happy, doing normal things a young girl my age should be doing. My mother was far more concerned about securing our Polish citizenship papers so we could leave Zhetel and return to Poland. She had to do it very discreetly due to my membership in the Pionieri.

My future lay in the bosom of my family, not in that of Mother Russia, and I was admonished to be tight-lipped about our plans. I could not tell my friends that we would soon be departing. It was hard not to tell anyone, especially Merele and my secret crush, Grisha.

Łódź

June 1945 – August 1946

In the spring of 1945, we secured our papers + moved to Łódz, Poland.

We travelled from Zhetel to Łódź on trucks after an emotional and tearful parting from Rivke, who we left behind with little Joseph. She was waiting for her husband and could not leave with us. Shortly after we returned to Zhetel, all the partisans and men who were able to fight, including Shael and his brothers, Yechiel and Ephraim, had been conscripted into the Soviet Red Army. There was still fighting to be done and a severe shortage of men to do it. The Joselewitz brothers were skilled fighters loyal to the anti-Nazi cause, very useful to the Soviet army.

The admonition of our Russian doctor friend to leave Zhetel was supported by the changing political geography. Zhetel was in territory that would soon be ceded to the Soviet Union as part of agreements negotiated by Winston Churchill, Franklin D. Roosevelt and Joseph Stalin at the Yalta Conference in February 1945. The agreements included the reorganization of postwar Germany and Europe, including redrawing the Polish-Russian border.

As holders of Polish papers, my family and I were eligible to be repatriated to Poland. However, once Moscow shut the border Rivke and Joseph would become Soviet citizens. My aunt had a short window of opportunity to join us and needed to make a difficult decision, quickly: stay and wait for Shael and face being Comrade Rivke in a Soviet republic, or leave and hope he came back before the clock ran out. I imagine my aunt was very torn. She decided in the end to leave Zhetel. And none too soon. She made the last train out before the borders closed.

City street, Łódź, mid-1940s.

COURTESY OF JEWISH MUSEUM FRANKFURT. ARCHIVAL SIGNATURE: 3435/108

Rivke left a letter for Shael with a Jewish family in Zhetel explaining the plan to him. Unfortunately for Rivke, the letter was never given to him. The family kept it and spread vicious lies about her, convincing Shael that his wife had abandoned him. In the late 1960s, he established contact with Rivke and wrote to her. When Joseph was in his twenties, Rivke told him that his father had passed away. Joseph never knew him but honoured his memory by saying Kaddish, the mourner's prayer said for eleven months after the passing of a parent and yearly on the anniversary of their death.

I was twelve years old when we arrived in Łódź. Our apartment was in a pretty building that shared a courtyard with several other buildings. It was located on Jednastego Listopada (11 November Street, named for the date in 1918 when Poland reclaimed its independence), well-situated off a main street filled with shops. The apartment was small but comfortable. To the best of my recollection, that is where I finally had my first proper bath in years. I cannot even imagine the colour of the water that went down the drain afterwards.

Anti-Semitism still raged in Poland and throughout Eastern Europe—and Łódź was no exception. We may have been liberated from the forest, but we were not yet liberated from persecution. A young girl who worked in one of the stores near us was killed in the courtyard of our building by the Armia Krajowa (Polish Home Army), known as the AK—a virulently anti-Semitic, nationalist Polish underground force committed to their slogan Polska bez Żydów (Poland without Jews). I wish I could say that her death was an isolated instance of post-liberation violence against Jews. Sadly, it was not. We knew of stories of murderous AK attacks on the survivor population even after liberation. Watching the perpetrators flee through the courtyard of our building left us with no illusions. It was clear we could not remain in Łódź any longer than necessary.

Rivke finally made it safely to us, and she and my mother became the breadwinners in our family. Joseph and I were left in the care of Bobe Hoda while my mother and aunt travelled all over Poland—and as far as Czechoslovakia—buying and selling goods in an effort to raise the 100,000 złotys to pay for our little group to get across the border to the west. That sum would be equal to U.S.$540 today, a huge sum of money at the time.

There are many questions I wish I had asked my mother after the war, one of which is whether my theory of how she and Rivke got started in their business venture is correct. Łódź was a centre for textiles, and I believe Mama and Rivke got back into the textile business with the help of an old "friend" of Uncle Chaim's. I have a recollection that when we returned to Zhetel after our liberation, my mother visited the gentile to whom Chaim had given all the bolts of our cloth for safekeeping just before we entered the ghetto. He was the man that Mama visited after we escaped, the one who told my mother to return later and arranged a Nazi welcome party for her that she noticed before falling into his trap. Mama accused him of being a collaborator, and I believe he may have given her back some of our fabrics to placate her. Unfortunately for him, he was already widely known as a Nazi sympathizer. I witnessed him being hanged later in Zhetel, together with other collaborators. And I remember feeling God was just.

I understood how important it was for Mama to be away, but I missed her desperately. All of her absences throughout our postwar displacement years were very hard. One time Mama returned from one of her buying trips with a rare treat—oranges. While she was away I had come down with a severe case of measles and was quarantined. Bobe was the only one who stayed with me, nursing me back to health. Mama's oranges were very sweet medicine.

Malka Bielski, who had been with us in the forest, was also now in Łódź with Yosef, Yisroel and her "forest husband" Yitzhak Rubenstein. They lived in one of the buildings around the same courtyard as ours. Malka was one of my early style influencers. She was very petite, with small feet, and I remember trying on her high heels, a beautiful pair of red pumps. "You should always wear heels, Chavale," she said. "Your legs look very good in them." I felt very flattered. I held on to her words like a secret promise that one day I would have heels of my own.

We were in Łódź for about nine months while Basia and Rivke set out to raise the money we needed to pay for our passage out of Poland. I was enrolled in a Jewish school, where I began learning Hebrew. I loved it. Since I had learned the alphabet while studying Yiddish in Lida—and both languages share the same one—I picked up Hebrew

Evelyn dancing, Łódź, 1947.
COURTESY OF EVELYN KAHN

quickly. Mama also found tutors for me, and life began to return to a semblance of normalcy. I had to travel a fair distance by tram to get to the school. I was so fearful of the enduring anti-Semitism that I sat in the back of the car so as not to bring attention to myself. I was also very careful to keep my Hebrew books out of sight, aware that we were not welcome in Łódź.

I was captivated by the self-confident Polish school girls who rode the tram with carefree abandon. I envied their beautiful uniforms and their lovely briefcases. I wished I could stop worrying about hiding my Jewishness and be just like them. Once I got to school, I also studied Polish and learned to speak it without a Yiddish accent. That helped me blend in on my commute. I felt comfortable asking for a ticket on the tram or going to the bakery. My sweet tooth was still intact, and my trips to the bakery to indulge it were my only other interactions with Poles. My favourite baked goods were still anything with chocolate.

I was fortunate to meet a lovely friend, Rina Burak, who became my emotional saviour. Rina had lost her mother after a neighbour of the Christian family who took in Rina and her parents betrayed them to the Gestapo. The shared experience of losing parents created an immediate bond between us. We did everything together in our spare time after school. It was to her that I confided when my body officially changed from girl to woman. Rina ended up moving to Paris. We corresponded for a time but lost touch.

I did my homework at the home of a school friend, Shael Razwaski. Shael was from Zhetel. He was about three years older than me and very good at maths. His half-sister Darlene later married a man from Zhetel named Mike Alpert; it was through Mike that Rivke learned that the woman to whom she had given her letter for Shael had kept it.

I started to sing and dance again. A group of survivors who lived in Shael and Darlene's building were professional entertainers, singers and actors. They must have heard me singing in school because they asked me to sing with them in a theatre. It was a performance for the survivor community. I was twelve-and-a-half years old, and I sang a version of a Yiddish song called "Papirosn" (meaning "cigarettes"), with lyrics changed to reflect deprivations during the Holocaust and a boy selling ration coupons in the ghetto.

Our home in Łódź was always full of Jewish survivors, transients passing through on their own journey to a new life. Like us, many were on their way west. Hoda served as their den mother, cooking for our guests, safeguarding their valuables and providing a clean place to sleep. I can still see them sleeping on the floor of our apartment, lined up like sardines just as we had slept in the forest. The survivors would thank my grandmother by leaving her a bit of money to pay for their stay.

One of the transients who passed through our home was a partisan from Eishyshok. His family had owned a dairy, the same one where I was taken to drink pure cream in an effort to fatten me up. He was the sole survivor. His name was Leon (Leibke) Kaganowicz—my future husband.

Leon told my mother that he had plans to get out of Poland illegally with the aid of the Bricha, the Jewish underground helping Holocaust survivors illegally reach the west and the ultimate goal, Palestine.

I have a recollection that my mother asked him to help us leave and offered to pay him but that he declined. It is also possible that she may have just asked Leon to get our funds to the Bricha so that we could go with them, too. I never knew the whole story. I only know that for whatever reason, we did not leave Poland with the help of the Bricha.

My grandmother and mother paid smugglers to get our family across the Polish-German border. Our meagre belongings were packed and waiting when word finally came instructing us to assemble together with a group of other survivors at the designated meeting spot. We were all loaded in the middle of a summer night onto three trucks. It would be a long and harrowing trip.

The Bricha

Bricha (Hebrew for "escape") was a Jewish underground movement that helped Holocaust survivors and other Jews escape Eastern Europe between 1944 and 1948. Begun as an effort to assist Jews fleeing Nazi persecution, it soon became the main vehicle for the postwar exodus of Jewish survivors from Europe. Bricha helped move 250,000 Jews, including 170,000 Poles across Europe to different exit points and begin their journey to Palestine. At the time, Palestine was under British Mandate rule, which imposed strict immigration limits. Bricha—with support of the Haganah (Jewish defense forces in Palestine) and the American Jewish Joint Distribution Committee (a Jewish humanitarian organization)—helped Jews reach their ancestral homeland in defiance of the quotas. After the war, Jewish soldiers from the British Army's Jewish Brigade helped transform Bricha into a coordinated smuggling network, laying the groundwork for Aliyah Bet, the clandestine sea immigration of Jews to Palestine and ultimately the creation of the State of Israel.

Leon (Leibke) Kaganowicz, 1945.
COURTESY OF EVELYN KAHN

Berlin

August 1946 – August 1948

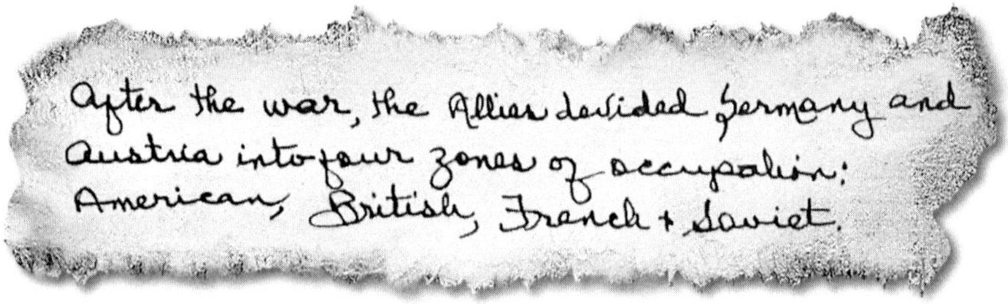
After the war, the Allies divided Germany and Austria into four zones of occupation: American, British, French + Soviet.

The Soviets occupied eastern Germany, along the Polish border. To get to any of the other Allied zones in Germany meant we had to cross the Soviet one. And we had to do so undetected by Russian army patrols. If they caught us, we could be sent back across the border or turned over to Polish security forces. We had no choice but to take our chances.

I do not know how long we had been driving or how far we had crossed into the Soviet zone before our convoy was stopped. Russian soldiers forced us all at gunpoint to disembark from the three trucks. We felt like we were back with the Nazis. Everyone was very frightened. We watched as the soldiers opened our suitcases and confiscated our belongings. They frisked each of us, man, woman and child, and took our valuables. I gave up a small ring my mother had bought for me. When they were through with their ransacking, they loaded the whole group together onto one truck. Fortunately, they did not send us back, and we were allowed to continue on our way.

Mirroring the division of postwar Germany itself, the city of Berlin was also split into four occupation zones. The Americans, British and French controlled the western sectors, while the Soviets controlled the eastern sector. (It was this sector that the Soviets walled off in 1961 with the infamous Berlin Wall, sealing off East Berlin from West Berlin—a barrier that stood until its fall in 1989.) I do not recall any further difficulties crossing through the Soviet occupied zone. I just remember that by the time our smugglers made us get out at the first stop—a transit camp in the French zone—we looked like we had come through a hurricane. I recall Rivke had only one shoe. We later found out that smuggling Jewish survivors was a thriving business. Worse, the team we had paid to take our group across the border were themselves Jews. They had cut a deal with the Russians and split all the plunder between them. As far as we knew we were the only group that was stopped and robbed. But I think that is unlikely.

Basia had known since we returned to Zhetel after liberation that there was no future for us in Europe. It was a truth shared by more than 250,000 other Jewish survivors of the Holocaust. Our common goal was to quit Europe and start a new life in a new country. For most, the dream was to immigrate to Eretz Yisrael (Hebrew, meaning "Land of Israel"), the ancestral homeland of the Jewish people. For the rest it was to immigrate to the United States, Latin America, Australia, South Africa, Great Britain or Canada. Wherever the final destination, the starting point for most survivors was a displaced persons (DP) camp in the postwar Allied-occupied zones. Most DPs would eventually be repatriated. But not all. Jewish survivors were among the group of "non-patriable" DPs, those who would not go back.

Rivke, Joseph, Bobe Hoda, Basia, and Evelyn, Berlin, 1947.
COURTESY OF EVELYN KAHN

Displaced Persons (DPs)

The term *displaced persons* (DPs) was broadly applied by the Allied powers to refer to people uprooted by World War II, an estimated fifty-five to sixty-five million people across Europe. They included civilians who had fled voluntarily, those forcibly deported by the Nazis, concentration camp survivors, prisoners of war, anti-Communists and even Nazis. The common thread: everyone had started the war in one place and ended it in another. By the war's end, in 1945, approximately eleven million of these individuals were classified as DPs, with six to eleven million of them in Allied-occupied Germany, including up to eight million in the western zones.

The Allies set up assembly centers and DP camps in the occupied zones of Germany, Austria and Italy, administered first by the United Nations Relief and Rehabilitation Administration (UNRRA) and later by the International Refugee Organization. These facilities were intended as temporary accommodations, as DPs were generally expected to return to their countries of origin.

And most did. Between May and September 1945, Allied military forces and UNRRA staff repatriated millions. Some returned voluntarily; others, especially in Soviet-controlled areas, were forcibly repatriated. Still, by the end of September, about 1.2 million DPs remained, mostly in the western zones of occupation—particularly in the southwest under U.S. control.

By 1951 the majority of these remaining DPs had immigrated to the United States, Canada, Australia and other destinations around the world.

In reality, it was not so much a case of would not but could not. We could not go back to our native countries. We had no homes to return to. We were permanently displaced. We were refugees. What we had was gone forever. Our communities had vanished.

Aerial view of central Berlin, 1945.

Our houses, towns, families and friends were gone. Many Holocaust survivors who returned to their hometowns voluntarily or through repatriation did not find a warm welcome. We heard the stories. Some found their homes were looted. Others found their homes had been appropriated by opportunistic neighbours sure that the Jewish owners would never return to claim them. The least fortunate went back and lost their lives, thanks to endemic anti-Semitism and anti-Jewish hostilities that had also survived the war. There were far too many stories of Jews who survived the Holocaust only to be murdered afterwards—like our young neighbour in Łódź and the forty-two survivors murdered in 1946 in the Kielce *pogrom* (a Russian word meaning "to destroy" or "wreak havoc").[1]

---

1 In July 1946, forty-two Holocaust survivors returned to the city of Kielce, in southeastern Poland, where they were murdered in a violent pogrom by local townspeople, police and soldiers that also left around fifty others wounded. The massacre shocked the world and shattered any remaining sense of safety for Jews in postwar Poland. In its aftermath, approximately ninety thousand to one hundred thousand Jewish survivors fled Poland for the west, many heading to displaced persons camps in Germany, Austria and Italy. Their arrival nearly doubled the number of Jewish DPs in the American and British occupation zones of Germany.

Arriving in Berlin when we did, in August of 1946, was probably a blessing for my family. A year earlier, our DP camp experience might have been far different.

It was not until fall of 1945 that circumstances finally changed for the better for Jewish DPs. The catalyst was the Harrison Report, which criticized the conditions of Jewish DPs and made recommendations to address their unique status and needs. Following the report, separate Jewish DP camps were set up and the American sector became known as the most welcoming to Jewish DPs from Eastern Europe.

The Harrison Report

In the immediate early days after the end of the war in 1945, Allied armies turned newly liberated concentration camps, like Bergen-Belsen, into camps for displaced persons, and conditions there were nearly as deplorable as in the concentration camps: overcrowding, barbed-wire fences and shortages of food, clothing and medicine. To make matters worse, the Allied armies initially grouped DPs according to nationality, so Jewish survivors were forced to live together with their persecutors. Survivors lived side by side with the very same Nazis and their collaborators—Germans, Austrians, Poles, Czechs, Hungarians and all the rest—who had made it their mission to murder them.

In the summer of 1945, U.S. President Harry S. Truman sent special envoy Earl G. Harrison to inspect the DP camps across Europe. Harrison was shocked by what he saw. In his report to Truman, Harrison famously wrote: "We appear to be treating the Jews as the Nazis treated them, except that we do not exterminate them." Thanks to him, Jewish DPs were recognized as survivors of genocide who required distinct recognition and care, prompting the U.S. and Allied authorities to improve camp conditions and create separate facilities for Jewish survivors. By the end of 1947, 184 Jewish DP camps and assembly centres existed in the American zone of Germany alone, housing about 185,000 Jewish displaced persons.

I can only speculate that my mother and grandmother had already learned in Łódź—via the survivor grapevine—about the Americans' relatively favourable disposition toward Jewish refugees. I believe that information prompted their decision for us to go to Berlin in the hope that we would be admitted to one of the two large Jewish DP camps in the American sector. One was the Düppel Center—also known as Schlachtensee, after the district and nearby lake—which housed more than 5,100 Jews, making it the largest Jewish DP camp. The other was Mariendorf, also referred to as Tempelhof, for its proximity to that district; it held around 3,250 Jewish DPs.

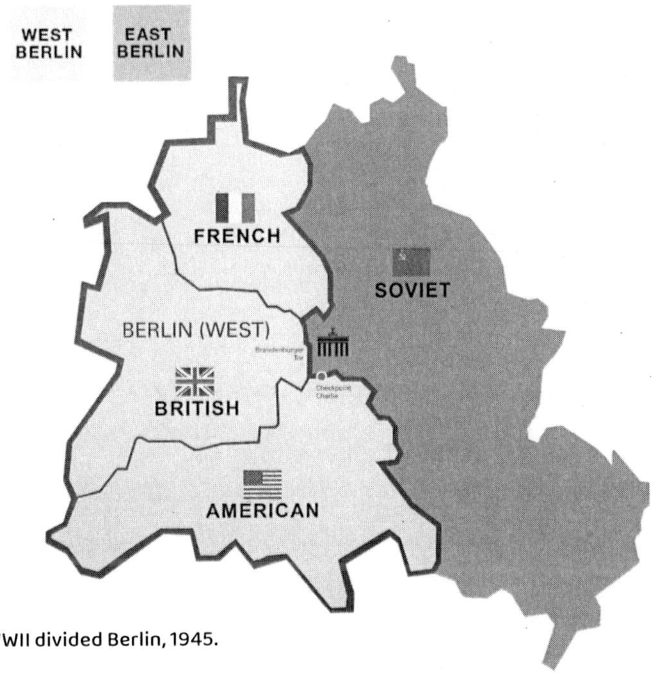

Post-WWII divided Berlin, 1945.

I think the plan to try for an American camp was probably a good one. But God was laughing again. Our journey to America began not in an American DP camp but in a camp in the French sector, where we were deposited by the smugglers.

The camp was called Wittenau, the name of the suburb where it was located. But I knew it as Eichborndamm, for its street address–Eichborndamm 140–148.

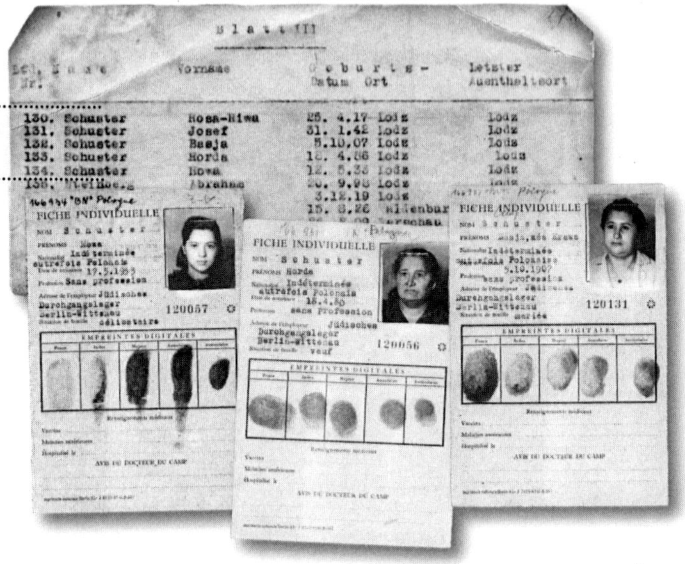

Berlin-Wittenau
DP Camp Registry
Berlin, 1946.

The Schuster family
130. Rosa-Riwa = Rivke
131. Josef = Joseph
132. Basja = Basia
133. Horda = Hoda
134. Howa = Evelyn

Family ID cards
from Berlin-Wittenau
DP Camp
Berlin, 1946.

Evelyn: Listed as Howa Schuster; stateless, unemployed; single
Bobe Hoda: Listed as Horde Schuster; unemployed; widow
Basia: Listed as Basja Schuster née Krawa; unemployed; married

COURTESY OF 3.1.1 REGISTRATION AND CARE OF DPS INSIDE AND OUTSIDE OF CAMPS, ITS DIGITAL ARCHIVE, AROLSEN ARCHIVES

It was the smallest of the Jewish camps in Berlin. My sense is that it was more of a transit camp. At its height, there were only thirteen hundred refugees in Wittenau.

We arrived at the camp in the summer of 1946, ragged and travel-worn, with only the clothes on our back and the few remaining scraps of our personal belongings that we had managed to salvage from the theft at the border. We looked a sorry sight. Fortunately, Wittenau's administrators took pity on our sad little group and admitted us to the camp. We were assigned to comfortable lodgings in a nice building that had once belonged to SS officers, an irony that was not lost on us. We may not have ended up at a more established American-run camp but as it turned out, there was an upside. Once we became acquainted with DPs in other camps, we confirmed that our accommodations were far more desirable than theirs. At Schlachtensee, for example, the accommodations were barracks and wooden huts.

Somehow during the intake process our names became somewhat scrambled, evidenced in the Wittenau DP camp registry for August 8, 1946. We are listed in the registry and in other documentation from that time under the family name Schuster (or Szuster) with the following first names: Horde, Rosa-Riwa (or just Rosa), Basja, Howa and Josef. (These misspellings would come to cause us a lot of anxiety in the future.) I think it is fair to say that our stay in Germany was a lot longer than any of us thought it would be. In total, we spent three years and three months in DP camps, including two years at Wittenau.

September 1944 may have been my liberation from the forest, but September 1946 was the liberation of my soul. As awful as I felt in Łódź, I felt exactly the opposite in Berlin. I felt secure. I felt victorious and not vanquished as I had in Poland. Berlin was my first experience since I was a very young child of being with my own people and truly feeling free. It was a positive experience for all of us but a little bittersweet for my grandmother. I remember walking with her in the city and her eyes tearing up as she remembered the words of her beloved Chaim, who had promised her we would all walk together in the streets of Berlin after the war.

My whole family was once again living together. Mama and Rivke had started to make a living as diamond merchants. I think they were part of a group of survivors that formed a consortium. Natural saleswomen, they were fast learners and very adept. It was not long before our family was able to afford healthy fare and new clothes. Bobe Hoda looked after Joe. They spent all day together. He had become very mischievous—maybe he was making up for lost time!—riding his little tricycle at considerable speed for a three year old, with Bobe, then age sixty, chasing after him. Other survivors often dropped into our apartment, and Hoda could enjoy some adult company—and respite.

My time in Berlin holds many dear memories for me. I still have friends today whom I met in Berlin and later reconnected with when I moved to New York in 1950. I met many through school. In Wittenau, there was a *Volksschule*, a small elementary school for young children, but not one for kids my age and certainly no local educational options my mother deemed suitable for me. Sending me to a German school was out of the question. So, she did what many other parents were doing with their school-age children, sending them to other DP camps, like Schlachtensee and Tempelhof, that had more educational resources. Mama chose Schlachtensee for me. It was the main centre of Jewish life in postwar Berlin and boasted rich cultural and religious offerings. It had schools for students in kindergarten through high school, a yeshiva, synagogues, and a Yiddish newspaper and theatre. The camp even had its own hospital, administration and police, as well as a court. It was here, at some point during our stay in Berlin, that there was a *din Torah*, a religious court judgment against our Jewish smugglers, and they were forced to pay my mother and the others in the group compensation.

I had to commute to school via the S-Bahn, Berlin's rapid transit railway, and change trains along the way. The S-Bahn had cars in first, second and third class. I always sat in the first-class car, waiting to be ejected. It never happened. I laugh now at my chutzpah. My mother eventually decided to board me with a widow living in Schlachtensee whose daughter Chayke was a few grades ahead of me at school. I slept on a little foldaway metal bed in their apartment.

My life settled into a new rhythm. During the week, I stayed in Schlachtensee and returned home for Shabbat. School ended early on Fridays and we only had Saturdays off. I began to have a more structured education. Schlachtensee aimed at preparing me, or so I thought, for life in Israel. I was thirteen years old now and in classes with other students my age. In addition to Jewish studies, Chumash, Jewish history and Hebrew, I also learned geography, maths, linguistics and Greek mythology. I still remember the lessons about Homer, Ulysses and Delphi. I started to learn English and French (which I liked better) during my summer vacation. My tutor's name was Ewa. She was very attractive and lovely and also very patient. Lessons with Ewa lasted only one summer, but thanks to her, when I arrived in New York in 1950 I had a rudimentary grasp of English.

Standing (l-r): Edek, Tzvi and Evelyn singing at Wittenau DP camp, Berlin, 1947.
COURTESY OF EVELYN KAHN

In addition to my studies, I also danced, sang and acted in school plays. All the plays were about the Holocaust.

One of the people who lived in our building at Eichborndamm was a 6-foot, 4-inch teddy bear of a man named Shaya. He was balding, with blue eyes and a ruddy complexion. He had a great sense of humour

Standing (l-r): Ruti, Rinata, and Evelyn, Berlin, 1947.
COURTESY OF EVELYN KAHN

Standing (l-r): Edek, Tzvi, Natan, and Evelyn, Berlin, 1947.
PHOTO BY MR. ROCK THAT APPEARED IN THE JEWISH GAZETTE AND THE LOCAL JEWISH NEWSPAPER, PROMOTING THE RECITAL. COURTESY OF EVELYN KAHN

and a wonderful personality. Shaya was a lot of fun to be around and the only one who could really make me laugh during that period. We used to swap canned goods from the packages given to us by UNRRA. He took my beans and I got his condensed milk, which we heated in the can to make caramel. I can still taste it. When I told Shaya I travelled first class on the S-Bahn, he told me that he did, too. And he took small revenge by taking off his shoes and polishing them against the plush velvet seats, in full view of the other passengers.

My social circle was a mix of friends from Eichborndamm, Schlachtensee, and my youth group. I remained friends with several after I left Europe, including Judy Kraus (Berkowitz), Masha Kagan (Seiden), Ruth Wagner (Koren) and Tzvi Blumenfarb. I lost touch with others completely, as their families moved to other camps and immigrated elsewhere. I also met three delightful girls—Rinata (Rina), Gisele and Ruti—when they came to Eichborndamm to collect packages from UNRRA. They would joke and say, "Wir sind Mischlinge (We are mischlinge)." *Mischlinge* was the legal term used by the Nazis to denote those with mixed Aryan and Jewish ancestry. It was rather fashionable for Germans to claim to be Jewish refugees in Berlin after the war. The three girls basically saw an opportunity to get free relief packages and clothing supplied by UNRRA. I remember cartons of clothing for DPs at Eichborndamm, and we got to choose a few items for ourselves. I picked a lovely jacket with a nubby texture in shades of browns and rusts, with a fur-trimmed collar and cuffs, and a pair of Oxford shoes that were very stylish. I loved the way they looked, but they fit very poorly. My feet were forever changed for the worse from wearing those shoes.

I was the group confidante, the repository of all the confessions and secrets of its members, especially between Gisele and two of my male friends from Eichborndamm, Edek and Tzvi. Sometimes the boys joined Rina, Gisele, Ruti and me when we went to the movies. Vitek, another boy from Eichbrondamm, knew I had a crush on the actor Stewart Granger, who was starring in a movie called *The Man in Grey*. He was very persuasive and convinced me to violate Shabbat to go to the movie with him. I confessed after the fact to Bobe and Mama, but they did not scold me. They never did. I was far too precious.

Evelyn in her Betar uniform, Berlin, 1947.
COURTESY OF EVELYN KAHN

There were no patisseries in Berlin as there had been in Łódź. There were only two choices for snacks, a *kneipe*, a pub, or a *bohnenkaffee*, a coffee shop. Rina, Gisele and Ruti were my introduction to these new establishments. Although there were no age restrictions for drinking, a kneipe held little appeal for me. I did, however, enjoy going to a bohnenkaffee for a strong coffee.

Ruti introduced me to her piano teacher, Herr Professor Doktor Linzel. Ruti was very talented, far more so than I. There was no piano where I was boarding, and, anyway, I was out of the house the majority of the time. I did learn to play, but not very well. The highlight of my short-lived career as a pianist was learning to play Johannes Strauss's well-known waltz, "Wiener Blut (Vienna Blood)." The girls spoke only German to me, which helped me master the language quickly and perfectly. I was assured I spoke without an accent.

My life in Berlin was very active. There were many Zionist youth organizations in Schlachtensee who vied to have us join their movement. The most popular ones were Gordonia, Hashomer Hatzair and Betar. *Madrichim*, counsellors from each branch, would make their spiel to us hoping we would choose to join their group. I joined Betar, possibly (probably) more to do with the very personable and cute *madrich* (male counsellor) than with the movement's tenets. Most of my school chums joined Betar with me.

Our Betar uniform was a white blouse and navy skirt. The blouses were given to us. We were also issued a boat-shaped hat that said Betar on it, and a small neck scarf with a pin that reminded me of my Pionieri uniform. We wore our own navy skirts. We learned Hebrew songs, marched with Israeli flags, had lectures, watched movies and went on field trips. All the activities were geared toward indoctrinating us and preparing us for *aliyah*, immigration to Palestine. I picked up Hebrew quickly and was passionate about my Zionism. Betar gave us back our Jewish self-esteem. A lot of us were drawn to the philosophy of Betar's founder, Ze'ev Jabotinsky, and to the poetry of Chaim Nachman Bialik. "To the Bird," ("El Hatzipor," in Hebrew) was a favourite poem of mine. By late 1947, many in our group had joined the Bricha's illegal aliyah groups.

Some of my most special memories of my two years in Berlin involved music. I will never forget the time I went with Rina, Gisele and Ruti to an operetta in a suburb called Charlottenburg. The suburb was restored after the war and is today beautiful and thriving.

It was easy and common for DPs, including us kids, to travel between the sectors to attend cultural performances in another zone. The operetta was in a theatre in the Soviet sector. I spoke Russian and was tasked with doing the talking at the box office. In spite of my shyness, I had a streak of daring and I wanted to impress my friends.

I calmly approached the ticket window to purchase the seats. Then, in a fit of outrageous audacity I spontaneously made up a story that my father was very good friends with the great Russian general Georgy Zhukhov, who at the time was Marshal of the Soviet Union, the country's highest military position. I have no idea what possessed me. But whatever it was it worked. We got prime loge seats, beautiful plush red velvet. The operetta we saw was by Franz Lehár. I do not remember the title, but I remember the overall experience. It was wonderful.

On one memorable occasion my entire school went to a symphony hall in Berlin to hear the world-renowned American Jewish violinist Yehudi Menuhin. Another time, I went to the state opera in Berlin. The music moved me deeply and I remember being completely mesmerized by the music and the voices. They especially resonated with me, as I had returned to singing and begun performing at recitals. Shortly after I arrived in Berlin a German man heard me sing in our compound and asked my mother if she would allow me to stay in Berlin to study voice on a full scholarship at a music academy there. I knew I could sing but did not consider myself that talented. I was very flattered, but it would have been a seven-year commitment. My mother, however, did not wish for me to be separated from her so I never took him up on his offer. To this day I do not know who he was, but I think he was an accomplished singer in his own right or connected in some way to the professional music world.

Many special people advocated for us during our time in the DP camps in Berlin, but there was one particular U.S. army chaplain, Rabbi Mayer Abramowitz, whom I remember with great fondness. Chaplains worked day and night to provide material and spiritual sustenance to displaced persons, and helped rekindle for us the flame of Jewish life. Lieutenant Rabbi Abramowitz was especially committed. He was young, amiable and very handsome. And he definitely kindled a flame in my teenage heart.

When I sang in his presence it was with great passion, as I felt like I was singing to him. Alas, Rabbi Abramowitz's own heart was captured by another survivor at Schlachtensee whose family had been deported from Poland to Siberia during the war. Her name was Rochele (Rachel) Kosowski, a lovely, intelligent "older" woman, as in older than me—she was twenty to my fourteen. The couple married in Berlin in November 1947. By coincidence, we ended up reconnecting in Miami Beach, Florida, when I was seated next to Rachel at a luncheon at Temple Menorah, the shul she and Rabbi Abramowitz founded there.

Rabbi Abramowitz remained a steady presence in Jewish DP (and my) life for the entirety of my time in Berlin. One Purim, I went on a retreat with my school to Schloss Brüningslinden, a palatial home outside Berlin we were told had been one of Hitler's getaways. We were all assigned to beautiful rooms and given costumes. Everyone dressed up. There was music and gaiety. And there was also the now-happily-married Rabbi Abramowitz. (His marriage had not dimmed my ardour. He was still my secret crush.) It was at that retreat my friends and I began to learn about American culture and social customs. Three specific and rather amusing lessons left an indelible imprint on my memory.

The first was the art of the cocktail party. I am not sure why this was deemed an important social skill to master. It does seem rather random, and there is some irony, given that many of us were under the legal drinking age in America. But apparently it was critical for our postwar success, so our adult mentors created a cocktail party for us. We were required to pick up a canapé and put it on a plate, take a napkin, hold a cocktail, circulate around the room and have a conversation. I remember hating this social custom. I found it very clumsy and challenging to have to manoeuvre all these items while walking and trying to find an interesting subject to make "small talk." To this day, I have no idea what small talk means. Perhaps a conversation about lice? They are small. All I know is that there is no intimacy at cocktail parties and they are my least favourite type of parties to attend or to host. I prefer the European way of sitting down at a table to dine properly and leisurely, while having engaging and meaningful discussions on a range of topics.

The second thing I learned that night was how to greet a stranger in America. This was a little more practical, as there were some cultural differences from the way Europeans greeted one another. I was taught that in America, you stand across from the person you are meeting and wait until they say "Hello" and introduce themself. Then you reciprocate by introducing yourself. You do not offer to shake hands

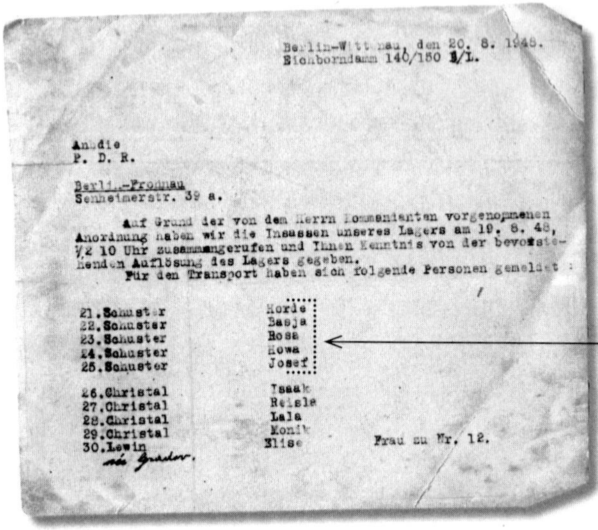

Berlin-Wittenau, den 20. 8. 1948.
Eichborndamm 140/150 3/L.

An die
P. D. R.

Berlin-Frohnau
Senheimerstr. 39 a.

Auf Grund der von dem Herrn Kommandanten vorgenommenen Anordnung haben wir die Insassen unseres Lagers am 19. 8. 48, 1/2 10 Uhr zusammengerufen und Ihnen Kenntnis von der bevorstehenden Auflösung des Lagers gegeben.
Für den Transport haben sich folgende Personen gemeldet :

21. Schuster Horde
22. Schuster Basja
23. Schuster Rosa
24. Schuster Howa
25. Schuster Josef

26. Christal Isaak
27. Christal Reisle
28. Christal Lala
29. Christal Monik
30. Lewin Elise Frau zu Nr. 12.

Wittenau closure announcement, Berlin, 1948.

Document translation:

Based on the order made by the commander, we called the inmates of our camp together on August 19, 1948, at 10:30AM and informed them of the impending dissolution of the camp. The following people have volunteered for the transport [...]

21. Schuster, Horde
22. Schuster, Basja
23. Schuster, Rosa
24. Schuster, Howa
25. Schuster, Josef

3.1.1 REGISTRATION AND CARE OF DPS INSIDE AND OUTSIDE OF CAMPS, ITS DIGITAL ARCHIVE, AROLSEN ARCHIVES

page - 2

	63677	149700	KOLODZIEJ	Anna	Ø	Pol.	r.c.	M	F	21.12.22	Kozlow/Pol.	housewife
	"	"	PYZIAK	Jozefa	C	"	"	S	F	8. 2.40	Kozlow/Pol.	child
35.	100909	149140	KUCZAK	Jozefa	X	Pol.	r.c.	S	F	20. 3.20	Miechowice/Pol.	farm worker
36.	"	"	"	Jozef	X	"	"	S	M	25. 8.42	Lahr/Germ.	child
37.	081296	156756	LIEPA	Aline	X	Latv.	prot.	S	F	14. 7.26	Linava/Latv.	student
38.	" 5	"	"	Olga	X	"	"	M	F	31. 8.98	Linava/Latv.	mother
39.	106882	161659	MALYK	Gregor	C	Pol.	gr.c.	M	M	12. 4.20	Hohoczy/Pol.	agricult.
40.	"	"	"	Maria	C	"	"	M	F	29. 9.14	Holhoczy/Pol.	housewife
41.	"	"	"	Irena	C	"	"	S	F	1. 2.43	Waldfischbach/Germ.	child
42.	"	"	"	Eugenia	C	"	"	S	F	19.12.47	Landstuhl/Germ.	child
43.	076752	160494	MATULIS	Roberts	X	Latv.	luth.	M	M	21. 8.09	Berzaune/Latv.	farm worker
44.	"	"	"	Anna	X	"	"	M	F	9. 9.05	Berzaune/Latv.	housewife
45.	"	"	"	Margers	X	"	"	S	M	4. 4.39	" /Latv.	child
46.	"	"	"	Jova	X	"	"	S	F	10.10.40	" /Latv.	child
47.	"	"	"	Ilse	X	"	"	S	F	15. 4.46	Saulgau/Germ.	child
48.	046604	175395	MOLNAR	Jules	C	Hung.	r.c.	M	M	13. 3.02	Budapest/Hung.	physician
49.	046603	"	"	Teresa	C	"	"	M	F	28.11.01	Debrecen /Hung.	physician
50.	"	"	"	Piroska	C	"	"	S	F	9. 4.38	Nyirghaza/Hung.	child
51.	"	"	"	Eniko	C	"	"	S	M	7. 9.39	Huszt/Hung.	child
52.	"	"	"	Eneso	C	"	"	S	F	9. 7.41	Ujvidek/Hung.	child
53.	087959	148304	MURASCHKINS	Sophie	X	Latv.	orth.	W	F	17. 4.12	Riga/Latv.	employee
54.	"	"	"	Tatjana	X		"	S	F	4. 4.38	Riga/Latv.	child
55.	94196	160115	OLSZEWSKI	Wladyslaw	S	Pol.	r.c.	M	M	11. 6.13	Wola Piekarska/Pol.	farm worker
56.	"	"	"	Helena	S	"	"	M	F	4. 1.25	Krasnodarsk/Russ.	housewife
57.	"	"	"	Helena	S	"	"	S	F	22. 4.47	Mullheim/Germ.	child
58.	100889	156530	SAWRAS	Stefan	C	Pol.	gr.c.	M	M	10. 6.24	Lemberg/Pol.	farming
59.	"	"	"	Maria	C	"	"	M	F	25. 9.22	Lemberg/Pol.	housewife
60.	"	"	"	Josefine	C	"	"	S	F	22. 2.48	Wurzach/Germ.	chil
61.	047058	166934	SCHUSTER	Rosa	X	Pol.	Jew	W	F	25. 4.20	Lodz/Pol.	housewife
62.	"	"	"	Jozef	X	"	"	S	M	31. 1.43	Lodz/Pol.	child
63.	47056	"	"	Basia	X	"	"	W	F	5.10.02	Lodz/Pol.	housewife
64.	"	"	"	Eva	X	"	"	S	F	17. 5.33	Lodz/Pol.	child
65.	047047	166934	"	Hoda	X	Pol.	"	W	F	18. 4.80	Lodz/Pol.	mother

Passenger manifest of USS *General Harry Taylor*, December, 1949.

61. Schuster, Rosa
62. Schuster, Jozef
63. Schuster, Basia
64. Schuster, Eva
65. Schuster, Hoda

3.1.1 REGISTRATION AND CARE OF DPS INSIDE AND OUTSIDE OF CAMPS, ITS DIGITAL ARCHIVE, AROLSEN ARCHIVES

unless the other person extends theirs first. In German culture, and in many European countries, the custom is to shake hands and make introductions simultaneously.

The last thing I learned was the concept of minding your own business. Maybe this was considered a survival skill. In America, we were counselled, if there is friction between people or they are in dispute, you do not interfere. We all found this advice rather amusing. In Europe, when you saw two people having an altercation in the street, you intervened. It took me years to understand that lesson. I guess I was a slow learner.

Rabbi Abramowitz and other Jewish officers in UNRRA and in the American Jewish Joint Distribution joined us for Shabbat (Hebrew for "Sabbath delight"), a gathering to welcome the Sabbath, and reintroduced us to Jewish traditions, including zmirot (Shabbat songs). The rabbi also organized a celebration when the State of Israel was declared on May 14, 1948. Listening on the radio as the UN vote was broadcast, we danced and sang and wept tears of joy.

Oh, how I yearned to go to Israel. But it was never really an option for me. Moving to the young state would have been difficult. We had no family there. Our family—Rav Yosef's sisters who had emigrated a few decades before my birth—was in New York. Mama had kept in contact with Rav Yosef's youngest sister, Chasya, who with the assistance of some of her nieces and nephews, was already working on affidavits to sponsor our immigration to the United States. As a result, I never realized my dream of living in our Jewish homeland. I always felt my soul lived in Israel, even if the rest of me lived in the Diaspora.

When we left Berlin, Rabbi Abramowitz and other American benefactors wanted to leave us with mementos of their time with us.

One of my benefactors, I believe his name was Mr. Auflager, unknotted the scarlette tie from around his neck to give to me. Another man, whose name was Mr. Rock, gave me a little handkerchief with a lace border and a small American flag in one corner. I still have the tie and handkerchief. The third gift was a pair of cufflinks from a man whose name I have forgotten.

Mr. Rock's handkerchief, Berlin, 1948.
COURTESY OF EVELYN KAHN

Mr. Auflager's tie, Berlin, 1948.
COURTESY OF EVELYN KAHN

Jordanbad to Gailingen to Landsberg to Bremerhaven

September 1948 – November 1949

Our time in Berlin came to a close in the summer of 1948, a consequence of the Berlin Blocade.

Earlier that spring, the Americans, British and French announced their plans to merge their occupation zones together to create a single unified West Germany. The Soviets responded with a blockade that effectively cut off West Berlin, and forced the closure of DP camps in the western sectors of Berlin, including Wittenau.

By the time we were forced to leave the city in September, there were fewer than 180 refugees left in Eichborndamm. Some survivors, particularly families with children, were able to sort their immigrated quickly before having to be resettled, and they managed to leave Germany for other countries. Because our family had originally been assigned to a camp in the French sector, when Berlin's DPs were evacuated we were obliged to go to another French sector camp.

Leaving Berlin meant a series of goodbyes to many friends. We all bought little journals in which we wrote farewell messages to one another. I still have my book. When I moved to New York in 1949, I reconnected with several friends who had immigrated to the United States before me and we rekindled our friendships there.

We were sent by train to Jordanbad DP camp, which had been a spa near Biberach in southern Germany. Jordanbad was a transit stop, meant as a temporary pause while we waited for assignment to our next camp in the French occupation zone. We were accommodated in a sanitarium run by Franciscan nuns that had been requisitioned by

Jordanbad DP camp, c. 1945.

COURTESY OF WIKIMEDIA AND NATIONAAL ARCHIEF

the French-occupying forces for use by the United Nations Relief and Rehabilitation Administration for the convalescence of concentration camp survivors and displaced persons. The town's citizens were quite indifferent to us, but the nuns were very caring.

Their kindness left a lasting impression, as did Jordanbad's pastoral setting. It was like a picture come to life. I loved walking through the countryside. It was there that I first saw cows with huge bells around their necks, walking and grazing in the meadows and making beautiful music. I am not sure exactly how long we stayed there, but I do not think it was very long.

From Jordanbad, we went 150 kilometres northwest to the town of Gailingen, in the state of Baden-Württemberg and just north of the German-Swiss border. You could literally see across the river to the town of Schaffhausen, Switzerland, famous for its watches. To my knowledge we were the only family from Berlin who ended up in Gailingen.

Gailingen was a far cry from big sophisticated Berlin. I remember it as the worst time in my life since the Holocaust. I developed an uncomfortable goiter there. It seemed to be an epidemic in the area. I saw many others with these large lumps on their necks below the Adam's apple. Goiters are a thyroid condition caused by iodine deficiency. They are preventable by the consumption of iodized salt, not common in Europe. I went to a doctor named Dr. Walters, who told me not to worry, that my goiter would disappear when I got to America.

And he was right. Iodized salt was plentiful in North America and my goiter eventually disappeared. However, I can still feel a small kernel of it to this day.

Like Wittenau, there was no formal education offered for me in Gailingen. The only option would have been for me to go to local German schools. But it was a non-starter. As in Berlin, my mother did not want me to go to a German school. And besides, we were not

The Berlin Blockade and the Beginning of the Cold War

The World War II alliance between the United States and the Soviet Union was one of necessity, not trust. Once the war ended, that fragile partnership quickly unravelled. The two emerging superpowers were divided by starkly opposing ideologies—Western democracy versus Soviet communism—and competing visions for postwar Europe. The Soviets wanted a weakened, divided Germany stripped of industry and burdened with heavy reparations, both as punishment and to aid Soviet reconstruction. The United States, by contrast, viewed a stable, economically strong Germany as essential for European recovery—and as a bulwark against Soviet expansion westward.

Tensions peaked in June 1948 when the Soviets sealed off all land, rail and water routes into West Berlin—effectively isolating more than two million residents from essential supplies, including electricity, food and fuel. The Western Allies responded with the Berlin Airlift—an unprecedented relief operation. Over the next eleven months, American and British aircraft made more than 270,000 flights, delivering more than 2.3 million tons of essential aid. It became the largest air relief effort in history.

Stalin's blockade failed to force the Allies out of Berlin. Instead, it crystallized a new geopolitical reality: the Cold War.

planning on being in Gailingen very long. Mama decided instead to rent an apartment in Landsberg am Lech, about 100 kilometres west of Munich, to make it easier for me to go to school at the DP camp there. I am not sure how she managed that, since we were registered in the French sector and the Landsberg DP camp was in the American zone. But she clearly figured it out because Hoda, Rivke, Joseph and I moved to Landsberg. I also began to study privately with tutors there, a lovely couple from Macedonia. Mama remained behind in Gailingen awaiting our exit papers.

Landsberg DP Camp

Landsberg was the second-largest displaced persons camp in the American-occupied zone of Germany. Located in Bavaria, it had previously served as a Wehrmacht military compound near one of the Kaufering subcamps of Dachau, where Jewish prisoners had been subjected to brutal forced labour. After liberation in 1945, the site was repurposed to house both Jewish and non-Jewish refugees, but it later became exclusively a Jewish DP camp. Landsberg is also notable as the town where Adolph Hitler was imprisoned in 1924 and began dictating "*Mein Kampf* (My Struggle)," the manifesto of his political ideology.

At its peak, Landsberg housed around five thousand Jewish survivors and became a hub of vibrant postwar Jewish life, with schools from preschool through university, a yeshiva, cultural institutions, a kosher kitchen, and the first *mikvah* (ritual bath) built in the American zone.

Landsberg was an organized and well-administered DP camp. It boasted many of the same amenities as at Schlachtensee and was likewise focused on preparing its DPs for Eretz Yisrael.

Like at Schlachtensee and Mariendorf, Landsberg had an ORT (Organization for Rehabilitation through Training) school, which provided short-term vocational training. For some, the trades they

Evelyn school photo,
Landsberg, 1947.
COURTESY OF EVELYN KAHN

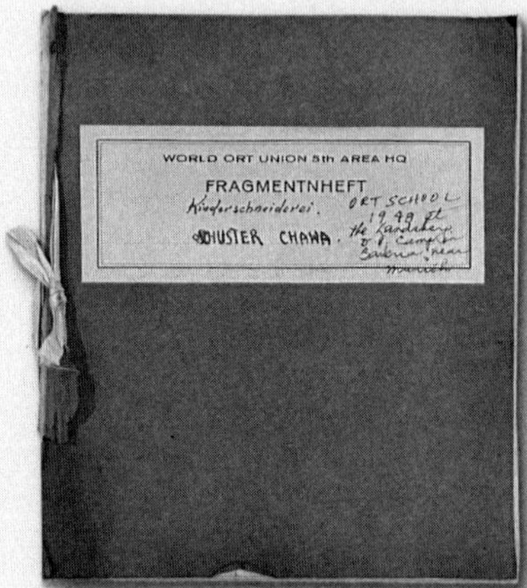

Evelyn's ORT school book,
Landsberg, 1947.
COURTESY OF EVELYN KAHN

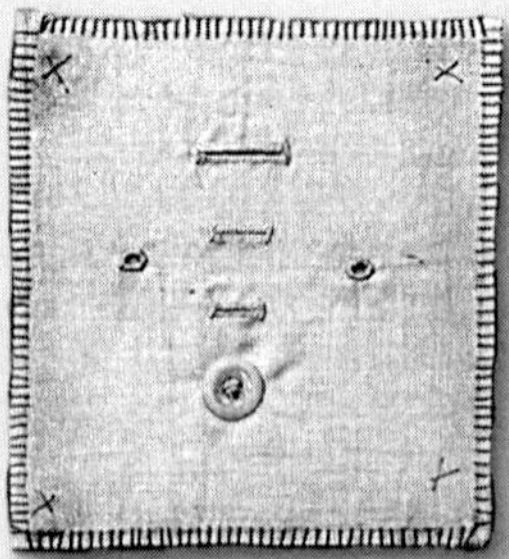

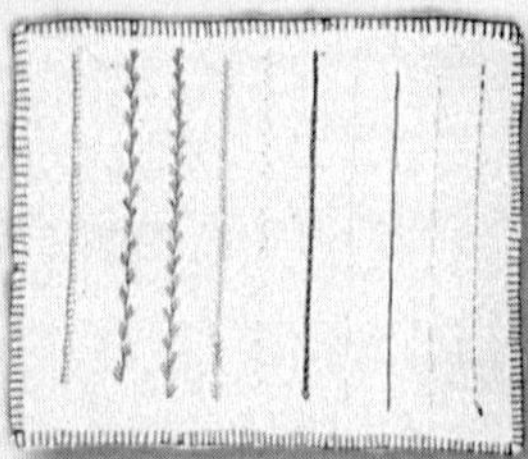

Evelyn's ORT school embroidery samples,
Landsberg, 1947.
COURTESY OF EVELYN KAHN

learned there helped with their emigration and later became their lifelong professions.

I learned how to sew and embroider there. I had mastered three different ways to attach a button and was hoping to become as proficient at embroidery as my mother, who was very skilled. I still have some of the handkerchiefs she made for me, as well as my scrapbook from that time with small samples of my own sewing and embroidery efforts. We left just before I began to learn how to use a sewing machine properly, but I have retained to this day the basic skills I learned at the ort school.

My friends Judy Kraus and Ruth Wagner, whom I had befriended in Berlin, had also moved to Landsberg with their families. Ruth was a year younger, a gap that melted away when we became adults. She remains a very dear friend. Judy and I briefly lost contact when she left Berlin, but we reconnected in Landsberg when my mother rented the apartment there and never lost touch after that. Judy immigrated to the United States a year before I did and wrote me letters from her new home in New York. She wrote in Polish and I wrote back in Yiddish. After a while, we decided to reverse the languages so we could each learn the other. We would encourage one another and correct each other's grammatical errors. Being multilingual, I imagined that I might one day like to be an interpreter for the United Nations. Although I never realized that goal, my arrangement with Judy proved very productive and successful for both of us.

I returned to Gailingen only twice during that period, both times in anticipation of emigrating. The first time was in the summer of 1949. But that visit turned out to be a false alarm; our papers had not been completely processed. The second time was in the late fall of 1949. I said farewell to my friends in Landsberg and returned to Gailingen until I left there for good. I prayed we would all reunite in New York, as I knew we were all headed in that direction.

The first step in making that happen was getting our American immigration papers. To do that, we had to travel to Singen, where the American and French immigration offices were located. My mother secured a car and driver and the five of us squished in. Singen is less than twenty kilometres from Gailingen. I am sure there are easier routes now between the two cities, but at the time the road we took was very narrow and winding.

We wended our way through mountain passes and I was very car sick on the ride, both from the twisty roads and the gas fumes that permeated our automobile. Overcome by the odour, my weak stomach finally revolted. We stopped once to let me be sick on the side of the road, and after that I had to use a bucket in the car. We had no time to stop. We had to be at the immigration office in Singen at a designated time, and it was critical that we get there at a specific hour or risk losing our interview. I felt completely disoriented and headachy by the time we got to our destination. I also felt guilty for delaying us.

We waited in the immigration office for what seemed like an eternity. There were many people ahead of us who claimed to be refugees. We wondered how many of those who sat with us for their turn at a new life were members of the killing squads of Poles, Lithuanians, Ukrainians, Estonians and Germans.

We were all in the same boat now. We sat on pins and needles waiting our turn, hoping things would go smoothly and we would get our papers. Finally, a French officer called us to enter his office. He spoke very little German and we spoke no French. We probably should have realized there would be consequences from this communication gap. But we naively relied on the clerk who was taking our particulars, assuming he was getting them down correctly.

Ever since living in Łódź, we had all been going by the same last name, my grandmother's. All five of us were registered at Wittenau under Schuster. We figured it would be less complicated. Up to that point, it had not been a problem. However, we were told by the immigration official that it was impossible for us all to have the same name. My mother did her best to untangle everything. She explained that her husband had been killed and that her married name was Landsman. She then explained the relationships of the rest of our family. The paperwork for our passports was completed, and Mama gave the matter no further thought. We received our documents and returned to Gailingen.

From Singen we returned to Gailingen to finish packing for our trip to America. We collected our belongings and took a train to Bremen, in northern Germany. Our final destination would be Bremerhaven, a large seaport where we would board a ship to the United States. We were in Bremerhaven for about ten days, during which time I met a lovely family, with two daughters and a son. The family's last name was Hamburger. Ironically, they were vegetarians, the first I ever met. The elder daughter, Ruth-Rosemarie, was around my age and we spent a lot of time together, going for walks and enjoying meals of eggs, bread and butter, and sharing our hopes and fears about what our new lives would be like in America. Hopes and fears seemed to be the standards of all the conversations among the survivors waiting in Bremerhaven then.

The passenger manifest for each ship in the seaport was posted on notice boards at the Bremerhaven Port of Embarkation and we went daily to check the lists for our names. Finally, Rivke's and Joseph's names appeared on a manifest, as did my grandmother's. Rivke and Joseph were listed as Joselewitz. Hoda was listed as Schuster. But where was my mother's name? And where was mine? They were both missing. How could that be? We had all filed our papers together. Panic crept in. Finally, after searching fruitlessly for the umpteenth time and not finding Basia or me on the list, Rivke asked my mother to see our passports. She thought she remembered seeing a different last name on our documents when she had briefly glanced at them. Sure enough, the last name on our passports was KRAWA.

So, Mama went back to check the passenger list and found Basia and Howa Krawa listed on the manifest for our ship. How we went from Schuster to Krawa is a mystery I will never solve. Thank God for my aunt. She always joked afterwards that we were now officially cows, which is the meaning of *krawa* in Polish. "What do you expect, Bashke?" Rivke teased. "You think they want Polish cows in America?" Interestingly (and confusingly) the ship's onboard manifest listed us all under Schuster.

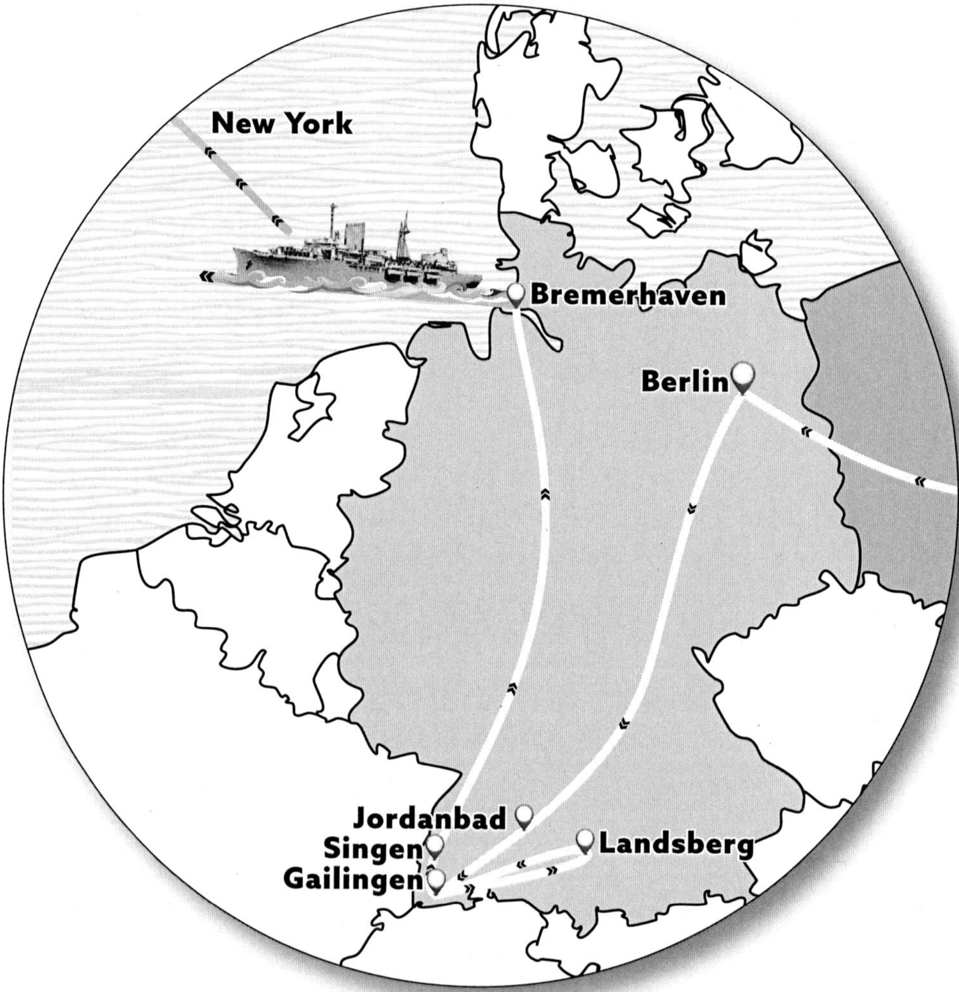
New York
Bremerhaven
Berlin
Jordanbad
Singen
Gailingen
Landsberg

PART FOUR
New World

New York

December 1949 – May 1953

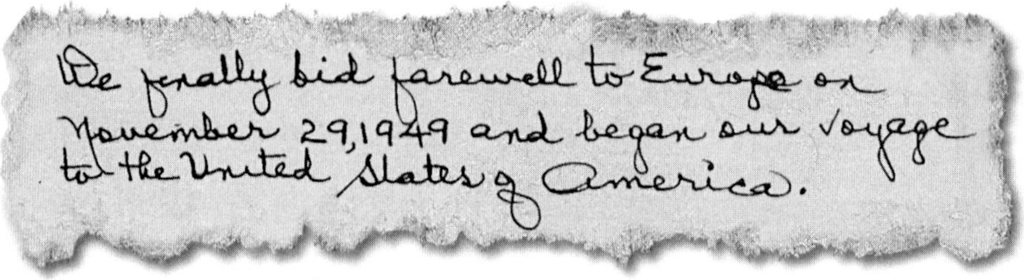

We finally bid farewell to Europe on November 29, 1949 and began our voyage to the United States of America.

We travelled with 1,267 other passengers, Jewish Holocaust survivors and other displaced persons from the war aboard a former transport ship named the USS *General Harry Taylor*. It was most definitely not a luxury liner. The ship was originally commissioned in 1944 to transport American troops, equipment and supplies for the war effort. Postwar, it had been converted to transport refugees for relocation in the United States.

Our accommodations were simple and spartan. My mother, grandmother and I shared one cabin. Joseph and Rivke had their own. Ours had triple bunk beds with metal frames, each with a thin mattress and woollen blanket. There was a communal bathroom down the hall, with a shower and toilets. Needless to say, with more than a thousand people to accommodate on the ship, lineups for bathroom facilities could be long. My family and I made do with sponge baths during the voyage.

USS *General Harry Taylor*, c. 1948.

COURTESY OF GARY PRIOLO NAVSOURCE / PROJECT GENERAL MANAGER / MANAGER, AUXILIARIES AND AMPHIBIOUS

One morning early in the journey, I looked into the ship's kitchen to try to make sense of the breakfast food. We had been served a new fruit I had never seen before, called grapefruit. Its acidity made me nauseous. I remember the butter was salted, unlike the unsalted and sweet European butter I was used to. There were also large loaves of sliced white bread. My family and I thought this bread more suited to cows. We dubbed it "cotton bread."

Though the accommodations were basic and the food strange, we were very happy to be aboard the USS *General Harry Taylor* that December. And very grateful. It was, all told, a memorable and special experience, also a novel one. The mood on the ship felt happy and optimistic, with a dash of anxiety mixed in. Everyone was going to start a new life in America, with a lot of unknowns. The Hamburger family was on our ship, which was wonderful for me. Ruth and I used to walk the deck, and with youthful naivety she and I assured one another we would maintain our friendship after the voyage, as we were both going to the United States. Little did we know how big the country was. Her family ended up in Tampa, Florida, and we did correspond for a time but we eventually lost touch.

My little cousin Joseph also loved exploring the deck. I or his mother would walk around the ship with him to keep him amused. Unfortunately, the fun stopped once we crossed the English Channel into the open Atlantic Ocean. On day three, everyone in our family started to get seasick. Everyone, that is, except my mother, who seemed as immune to seasickness as she had to all the sicknesses in the forest. I sometimes wonder if she simply willed herself to stay healthy all those years because we all depended so heavily on her. She could not afford to get sick. She was the chief caregiver to the rest of us. Mama used to bring us the white bread from the dining room, and hot consommé, but just a glance at it was enough to make me and the rest of us nauseous. I was so sick the doctor in the ship's infirmary had to give me an injection. He promised that as soon as I landed in New York I would be fine. He was right.

The crew on board the ship was very friendly and on the ninth day of the voyage, they let us know that we should go out to the deck. We could hear other passengers on the ship chattering about something important as well. It was freezing outside, but out to the

deck we went. The sight before us has remained with me all these years—the towering copper sculpture with its familiar green patina: the Statue of Liberty. As we passed Lady Liberty, with her torch and crown, we were all very moved. We could all relate to the words from Emma Lazarus's poem, which I knew courtesy of some of the other passengers and crew, who taught me what was inscribed inside the statue's base. "Give me your tired, your poor, your huddled masses yearning to breathe free." I was in awe as we drew closer to the dock and could not stop staring at Lady Liberty until we had anchored in New York Harbor.

We arrived in Manhattan on December 10, 1949. After washing as best we could and preparing ourselves to disembark, we assembled on the crowded deck and waited our turn. As much as I looked forward to getting off the ship, I felt fearful of the unknown.

Once our names were called, we walked down the gangway. I can still see myself leaving the ship, long hair tied back and wearing a navy dress my mother had made me, with a stylized white "EL" monogram on the front; warm white knee socks, navy suede shoes and a coat from UNRRA. We went to the luggage area to collect our small valises, and my mother made arrangements for three huge crates we had brought with us to be forwarded to the home of a cousin. The crates were filled with our household possessions, including fine European china and crystal Bobe and Mama had bought in Berlin and somehow managed to bring with us from there, as well as other gifts for our relatives. After the disposition of the crates was sorted, we proceeded to the enormous immigration hall. It was in a large, nondescript building teeming with people, all of whom seemed to blend in my mind into one giant mass of humanity. We waited a very long time in line, holding down our anxiety as we inched very slowly forward to the long tables behind which sat dozens of immigration officers. Finally, we reached the front of the line and it was our turn. Our papers were carefully checked and stamped, and we were cleared for entry to the United States. Our journey was over. We had arrived.

My great-aunt Chasya (née Schuster) Paley, who had been the driving force behind bringing us to America, was the only one of my grandfather Rav Yosef's sisters who was alive when we got to New York. We longed to see her, and she felt the same. As the sole survivors of her late brother's family, we knew how precious we were to her. But what about the rest of Rav Yosef's American family? We were hopeful they felt the same, but we were very anxious about them. We were about to find out.

Waiting to greet us at the dock were three cousins: George Rosenstein and his two sisters, Bertha Goldstein and Anna Cahane. It was to Anna's home that we had sent our crates. These cousins were three of the seven children of Chasya's older sister Guta Leah and her husband, both of whom had passed away before we arrived. Guta Leah was clearly very revered by her children. Three of them named their daughters Gertrude, after her. Rav Yosef's second sister, Basia Bayle Schuster, who had immigrated to America with her sisters and their husbands, had never married. She had also passed away by the time we arrived in New York.

I am not sure how our cousins were able to pick us out of the mob at the dock, but I am guessing Bobe Hoda must have sent Chasya our pictures, perhaps the ones we had used for our immigration papers. The welcome they gave us was very warm. I put my rudimentary English to work. They were very complimentary and we passed inspection. Cousin Anna explained that we would be accommodated at the Hotel Beacon at Broadway and 75th Street, which was close to her apartment on Manhattan's Upper West Side.

Over time, we came to know all the members of the colourful and quintessentially New York family. And we developed relationships with nearly all of them. We would also develop affection for each of them—to greater and lesser degrees.

Each of Chasya's nieces and nephews seemed, at least to our family, to be remarkably successful in his or her own right. George was the eldest, a corporate lawyer turned circuit court judge in New Jersey. Next came Harry, a physician, Max, a lawyer, then Anna, who was married to Harry Cahane. The Cahanes lived very grandly on Manhattan's Upper West Side and were part of New York's social elite. Their daughter, Trudy, was on her winter break from school when I arrived in New York, so Anna invited me to stay with them for a bit. The formality of the Cahane home made me uncomfortable, but it was stunning and stirred in me what would become a lifelong passion for interior design. I remember walking into my cousin's beautiful prewar apartment for the first time and seeing crates that Mama had arranged to be delivered to Anna's arriving upstairs in the private elevator that opened into the apartment. My mother oversaw the unpacking of them by Anna's household staff. "Take what you like, Anna," my mother said to her. "Everything is for you." And she did.

Anna's younger sister, Bertha, was the family "underachiever." She was "only" a secretary. Fortunately, she married a dentist, Louis Goldstein, a kind man who was easier to love than Bertha, who could be a bit overbearing. (Our nickname for her was the "*kochleffel*," from the German word for wooden cooking spoon. She was always stirring the pot.) The couple did not have any children of their own, but Bertha had a daughter from a previous marriage whom Louis treated as his own. Her name was Gertrude. And she also went by Trudy. Shortly after I met her she told me she had just celebrated her sweet sixteen.

I had no idea what she was talking about, even when she showed me her fancy corsage. But I played along. She and I became lifelong friends in spite of her mother, who was not keen on her daughter and I becoming too close.

Albert was the second-youngest Rosenstein. He and his wife came once to inspect his specimen cousins from Europe. I guess we satisfied their curiosity enough in only one meeting because we had no contact with Al after that single encounter.

Asa Rosenstein was the youngest of Guta Leah's seven children. He was my favourite and also the favourite of the family. Like his older brother Harry, Asa was also a doctor. He and his wife, Beatrice lived not far from us in the Bronx. Beatrice was a pianist and a lovely woman whom I admired very much.

My great-aunt Chasya's life was in sharp contrast to that of her nieces and nephews. Charitable and selfless to a fault, my great-aunt was the definition of a *tzadekes*, a righteous person. She was one of those souls who felt she was just a visitor passing through this world. She was ready to depart at any time. I remember she even had her tachrichim prepared for when she died. Chasya lived at 400 E. Houston Street, Apartment 14, on Manhattan's Lower East Side. She sold Judaica and had a little grocery store that catered to the small Jewish community in the neighbourhood. If she took in ten dollars, she would put aside a dollar for charity. My family and I went to visit her a few days after we settled into the Beacon Hotel. Hers was the first New York walk-up apartment we saw. It was about 400 square feet, on the second floor of a small apartment building. Paint was peeling off the wall. There were few pieces of furniture: a little sofa, a small table and one dining chair. In one corner was a cot with an iron frame. There were maybe three or four plates, a few pieces of cutlery and one mug in the tiny open kitchen area. We were terribly distressed when we saw the conditions in which she lived and how she neglected her health. It was all so depressing that we soon stopped going to her and instead she would come to us.

I was sixteen and a half years old when I landed in New York. It was the Christmas season and the city was very festive. Decorations and Christmas lights were everywhere, making Manhattan's streets come alive with holiday cheer. I remember around mid-January, after all the decorations were removed and the lights taken down, there was a sadness in my soul. I missed Europe and all my friends there. But it was something more. I did not really understand it at first. It took me a while to figure out that all those decorations were temporary. After the holidays were over and they disappeared, it was like a curtain had been drawn back on the real New York. I remember feeling hemmed in by the proverbial "concrete jungle" of the city. The subway was congested and dirty. The skyscrapers seemed to block out all the sun. And I missed the space and natural beauty of the landscape of Europe's cities.

My family was at the mercy of the benevolence and support of our cousins. We could not stay in a hotel forever. Anna and Bertha found us an apartment on the upper floor of a two-storey walk-up, built in 1901, at 2191 Ryer Avenue in the Bronx. The owner was a Jewish doctor who had an Italian wife. We were very excited by the prospect of moving into our own home. But our elation was short-lived. The apartment was furnished with an ugly, eclectic mix of hand-me-downs. Clearly, my cousins thought these cast-offs were more than suitable enough for their lowly refugee relatives. I remember our dining table in the kitchen had a cheap laminate top with a chrome base, and the rest of the furnishings were likewise unattractive. But in spite of the shabby decor, I never felt shabby.

The bigger disappointment came when my grandmother hoped Chasya's nieces would find work for Basia and Rivke in the Garment District, in one of the large Jewish-owned garment or textile factories, where Yiddish was widely spoken. Instead, they were placed in a small factory making costume jewelry on Manhattan's Lower East Side. Neither was suited to the work or very enthused, but beggars cannot be choosers.

For many survivors, America was the *goldene medina*, the golden land, because nearly anything seemed an upgrade from their simple shtetl life. For us it was exactly the opposite, an unwelcome and uncomfortable downgrade. For me, the transition was also emotionally painful. It was in New York that I truly felt the absence of a father. I also especially felt the absence of a husband for my mother, someone who could help share and lessen her burden. I did gradually grow to find my place in New York. But not completely.

Bobe Hode, Ryer Avenue, Bronx, NY, 1950s.
COURTESY OF EVELYN KAHN

Basia and Rivke, Ryer Avenue, Bronx, NY, 1950s.
COURTESY OF EVELYN KAHN

Our neighbourhood was a mix of mostly Jews and Catholics, Irish and Italians, a veritable melting pot of immigrants to America. Some, like ourselves, were fresh off the boat. It was around this time that my mother Americanized her name from Basia to Bessie, and Joseph began to go by Joe. Another change was that Mama and I became less Jewishly observant. We were still very traditional and culturally Jewish, but we no longer observed Shabbat as strictly as we had in Eishyshok. My grandmother, on the other hand, remained steadfast in her Jewish observance. She continued to go to shul every Shabbat and ensured that our home remained strictly kosher. She also never learned more than a little English. In her world, Yiddish was the lingua franca.

Bertha enrolled me at Walton High School, a prestigious all-girls public high school located in the Bronx. Not only was the school new for me, so was my name. I was now Evelyn, thanks to the ever-officious Bertha. Cousin Joe started grade one in a public elementary school across the street from our apartment; however he was there only for a short time. Rivke had remarried, to a man named Melach Gordon, a year after we moved to the Bronx, and she and Joe had moved with her new husband to Freehold, New Jersey. After they left, we took in a boarder named Herschel Portnoy to help with the rent. Herschel was also a survivor and was a tailor by trade. He made me a beautiful suit with fabric my mother bought on the Lower East Side. It had a skirt and a long one-button jacket in a beautiful shade of blue.

Walton had thousands of students. It should have been a good fit. The school had many students from immigrant and working-class families. But I, the newly minted Evelyn Landsman, felt lost among them. I was a new immigrant but felt very foreign there. I did not realize it at the time, but I guess the environment was just too elitist for me. The school was very academically oriented, and I had no idea how to choose subjects that might have been more suited to my natural abilities or that would have allowed me to develop more practical skills. I was very green and had no friends and no one to talk to. And worst of all, I had been put back several grades.

School was very hard for me, but there were two teachers at Walton who were exceptionally kind. One was Mr. Rossi, my history teacher. The other, whose name I have forgotten, was a Jewish maths teacher who knew about survivors. In one of those small-world stories, she showed me a photo from a local German-language Jewish newspaper of me singing in Berlin with Natan, a friend from Eichborndamm. It turned out that the photo was taken by Mr. Rock, the man who had given me the little embroidered handkerchief when I left Berlin. The teacher asked me if I would like to sing a solo with the choir. It was a huge choir and I declined because I still felt self-conscious. Furthermore, I did not know any songs in English and was afraid to sing in Hebrew or Yiddish.

It was during that period I met Frieda Haber, who became a dear and lifelong friend. It is a source of humour to us that neither one can remember how we met. A small detail. I just remember she also lived in the Bronx, and she was approachable and kind. Frieda was a great source of support and comfort to me. Her home became like my own. Frieda was also a survivor. She had an innate understanding of our shared experiences. She and her mother had been saved by gentiles and her father had survived Auschwitz. I never learned all the details of her story. Frieda and I did not dwell on the past. We communicated soul to soul, without words.

It was Frieda who told me about Roosevelt High School, which was much closer to where I lived and within walking distance of my home. When I inquired about transferring to the school I was told they would give me many credits for my schooling in Europe, including credit for Hebrew. Plus, I would be placed in Grade 11, which was the right year for a student my age and gave me a much better chance of graduating with my cohorts. I finished the semester at Walton and transferred to Roosevelt in September 1950. I am not sure why, but when I moved to Roosevelt I was back to being Howa Krawa, the name on my immigration papers.

Evelyn, graduation photo, Roosevelt High School yearbook, Bronx, NY, 1952.
COURTESY OF EVELYN KAHN

In Germany I had been a capable student and very confident in school. But in the United States my English lagged and I was not in my element. I felt small. The only subject where I did not feel diminished was history. It was (and still is) my favourite subject. When the history teacher asked who was the prime minister of France, I was the only one who knew the answer. The American kids were lucky if they knew their own history, let alone that of Europe.

My history teacher, who was Jewish, later became a source of great disillusionment and pain for me. I had taken a big history exam and he took me aside afterwards and told me he had not passed me. Worse, he accused me of cheating on the test! Me, a cheater! On history, my best subject. I was crushed. I was not raised in a family with confrontation and I did not know how to advocate for myself. I was afraid that I would break down as I tried to tell him that I was innocent. I was over-sensitive and kept all my distress to myself. Because of him

I never graduated high school with the rest of my class. And I never went back to finish. Ironically, the school yearbook was compiled months before the end of the school year. So my photo is included in the graduating class of Roosevelt High School's 1952 yearbook, listed there as Howa Krawa.

A friend of my mother's recommended to her that I should go to secretarial school. The cost was a few hundred dollars—an enormous sum and a huge economic hardship. It is a trauma to me to this day because I learned after the fact that Roosevelt had more than just the traditional academic track. There was one that was geared to trades. I would have been able to learn secretarial skills for free at school, instead of my mother having to pay for tuition at a secretarial college.

When I completed the secretarial course, I got a job taking shorthand and writing business letters at the costume jewellery factory where Rivke and my mother were working. When I was let go by that company I found a new secretarial position at a seniors' home. I had always lived with my grandmother, so I found it natural to engage with older people. I liked the older adults at the home and enjoyed eating lunch with them. But the overall atmosphere there was very cheerless. Part of my job entailed writing letters on behalf of the home to the families of the residents. I remember being very troubled by those letters. It was my first exposure to the stark difference between European and American culture in the way the families treat—and neglect—their parents. There was no sense of filial responsibility. The children were happy to outsource the care of their parents to caregivers. As much as I enjoyed the residents, I found the job depressing.

Fortunately, a co-worker of my mother's connected me with a survivor in the garment industry who hired me as his secretary. My salary was fifty dollars per week. When I got my first week's paycheque, I told Judy, "I feel very rich!" It was a wonderful feeling, and my biggest pleasure was giving the money to my grandmother. Bobe managed the household and I was in heaven that I could truly contribute to the family now and still have a little money to spend on myself. The first thing I bought was a $4.99 pair of navy suede sandals with a high heel. The second thing I bought was a navy skirt with a white stripe. It was the happiest time in my working career.

Soon after I moved to the Bronx, Judy, Frieda and I started to go to social events and dances together. There were lots of dances for us "greeners," the colloquial term for new immigrants. The dances were held in beautiful venues. I loved to dance and always had a good time out with my friends. It was at one of those dances, held at a little night club, that I sang in English in public. I sang "Kiss of Fire," a song made famous by the popular American singer Georgia Gibbs, who I later found out was a nice Jewish girl whose real name was Frieda Lipschitz.

One of the biggest social events was a dance held on Purim. The 1950 event was particularly memorable for me, as I was chosen as Queen Esther. The following year on Purim I was one of the judges for the dance contest.

In May 1952, I went to another dance in the same venue. I came with my mother on that occasion. She saw a familiar face coming through the entry doors of the dance hall. It was Leon Kaganowicz, the young man she had last seen in Łódź when he passed through our home there after the war. He was in New York visiting relatives. My mother headed toward him, and when she reached him asked if he remembered her. He did. He then asked after Bobe Hoda, saying he would like to visit her.

My mother then said, "Do you remember my kleine Chavale (little Chava)?" Leon said sure, and pointed to one of my friends. Not surprising, since he had last seen me when I was about eleven years old (and he had arrived at the dance a bit tipsy). Fortunately, the correction was made. This chance encounter would change my life.

True to his word, Leon came to visit Bobe Hoda, and I happened to be there. He asked me if I would like to go out with him. In truth, I was not attracted to him at first. He seemed a lot older than the boys in my circle, who were much more boyish and felt younger and more carefree. It did not help that he sported a very short cropped haircut that aged him and was not particularly flattering. But my mother said I should go out and show him the town. So I did.

Our dates included two concerts, one featuring the popular singer Joni James and the other the husband-wife duo Les Paul and Mary Ford. We also went to Radio City Music Hall and saw the film *Kiss Me Kate*, with Kathryn Grayson and Howard Keel. We dined out at diners. And we liked one another.

Leon's photo, with inscription to Evelyn, Vancouver, BC, 1952:
"To my dearest, Evelyn. The girl I intend to marry, and love for the rest of my life,
Leon Kaganowicz."
COURTESY OF EVELYN KAHN

My mother and my bobe encouraged me in the relationship despite knowing it could end up taking me far away from them. After our three-week courtship, Leon and I decided to write to one another. He said if we still felt the same about one another after writing for a year, we would get married. But my mother told him that if I were somehow beholden to him during that year, I could not go out with other boys. The implication was clear. So before he left we got engaged. Leon sent me a one-carat diamond solitaire ring by mail that he had been keeping since Germany. My mother sent him a huge box of diamond-shaped *pirozhki*, little hand-pies she stuffed with honey and poppy seeds and boiled in honey until they were golden brown—an edible dowry. The deal was sealed.

Leon and I did write for that year. You put your best foot forward during courtship, especially a long distance one. Our letters were very sentimental but serious. We planned our lives together not really knowing one another. I remember we used the word "gratitude" a lot

Evelyn's photo, with inscription to Leon, New York, NY, 1952:
"To dear Leon, the fellow I intend to love for the rest of my life, Evelyn L."
COURTESY OF EVELYN KAHN

in our correspondence. I think what made us bond was that we had the same background and a shared culture. We also had the same goals and aspirations: to live a full life, to have a family and a little home complete with the proverbial picket fence.

One of the bonuses of meeting Leon was getting to know his wonderful cousins. When Leon's step-uncle, Aron Don, whose last name was Pacianko, had arrived at Ellis Island he was unable to convey the proper spelling of his surname to the immigration officer. After numerous failed attempts the exasperated agent finally asked Aron Don what he did for a living. Aron Don responded in Yiddish that he was a *becker*, a baker, and the family's last name was changed that day to Becker. I was very close to the Becker children, especially to Bessie and her husband, Max, who became like second parents to me. Most of my relatives, by comparison, were more like Santa Claus. After Christmas 1949, they seemed to disappear—except Bertha the kochleffel, the pot stirrer.

My mother and grandmother and I wanted a big wedding. I was a gift to my mother, an only child and a survivor of the Holocaust. Mama believed my wedding would be an expression of how her daughter would be provided for. Leon knew my mother had limited means, but Basia was not one to ask to split the cost. In truth, she could not understand why a person of Leon's age was not able to save anything for himself. From his side, he was a sole survivor who needed only to sustain one person. In the end, my mother told him that she would pay for the majority of the wedding.

Leon and I were married on May 23, 1953, in a wedding hall in the Bronx. We had been mindful of expenses and kept our expectations modest, which was fortunate since the wedding had some hiccups. A cousin of Leon's offered me the bridal gown their daughters had worn at their own weddings. I took it to a dressmaker friend of my mother's, who lived in the Bronx and was married to a man from Eishyshok.

The dress was altered, but when I went to put on my gown a few hours before the wedding, it was hanging on me. I had lost a lot of weight from pre-wedding stress and never had it refitted. I put safety pins inside the bodice to make it fit. My hair was another story. I had gone to have it trimmed before the wedding and it was cut too short, especially the bangs. To top it off my headpiece kept falling off my head. I chose flowers that were way too big and totally wrong. I was not discriminating in my tastes then. I have come a long way. I joked with Leon that I wanted to have another wedding.

Cousin George Rosenstein and my mother walked me down the aisle. Leon's cousins Max and Bessie Colodzin walked Leon. My cousin Joe was the ring bearer.

We received three thousand dollars in cash, a healthy sum, as well as some lovely gifts. Max and Bessie gave me silver-plated cutlery. They also gave us the precious gift of their sage and wise counsel as Leon and I navigated the choppy waters of our early marriage. They helped me understand the challenges of growing up without a male figure and Leon without any family, and the impact on him of the trauma of losing them.

Hoda spoke no English, and it would have been hard for her to move to a place without the kind of support she had in New York. The Bronx was like a small shtetl. She managed perfectly fine with no English there.

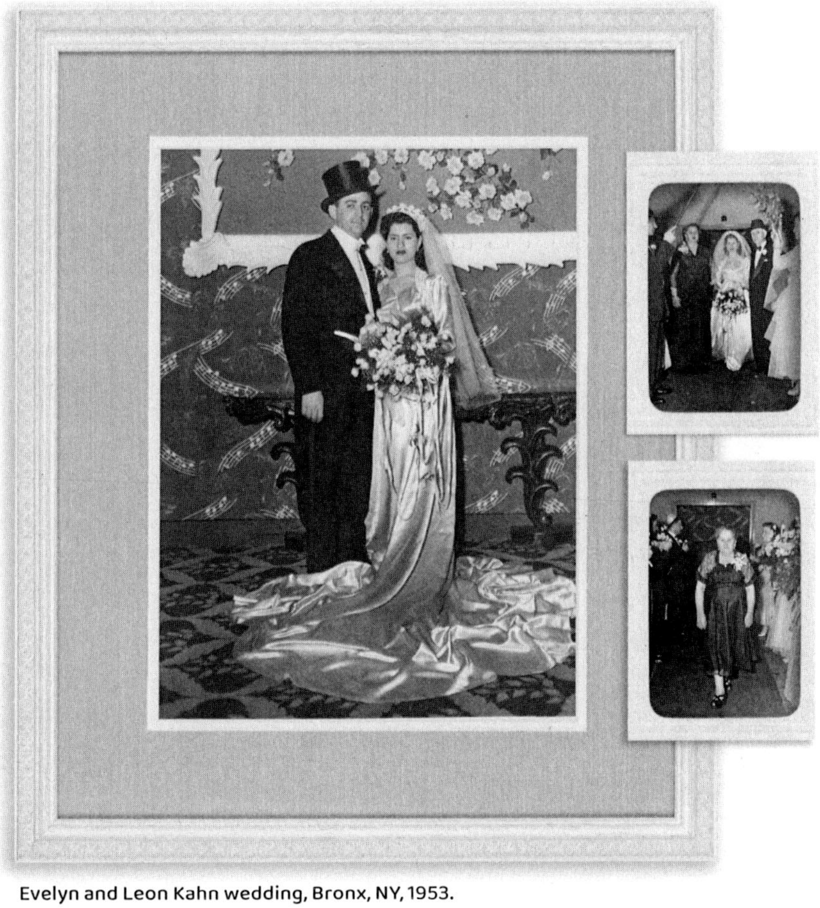

Evelyn and Leon Kahn wedding, Bronx, NY, 1953.
COURTESY OF EVELYN KAHN

Evelyn and Leon, newlyweds, Vancouver, BC, 1953.
COURTESY OF EVELYN KAHN

Evelyn and her young family
(l-r): Mark, Evelyn, Hodie, Leon and Saul, Vancouver, BC, 1962.
COURTESY OF EVELYN KAHN

Letting go of my mother and grandmother was crushing for me. My parting goodbye was very painful. I learned later my mother was not only heartsick but physically ill for a time after I left New York.

After the wedding, we stayed for a few days in midtown Manhattan at the luxurious Hotel Astor, a beautiful beaux-arts hotel on 42nd Street, before embarking on our honeymoon to San Francisco. The hotel had a lovely roof restaurant with dancing that was popular with the society and celebrity set. I saw the actors Janet Lee, Tony Curtis and Jerry Lewis there.

From San Francisco, we took the Northern Railway Empire Builder train to Vancouver. I was very taken with the scenery I could see through the glass of the observation car. Just as I had felt when I saw the Statue of Liberty, I became very emotional as we crossed the U.S.-Canada border. The caption on the American side of the giant Peace Arch monument on the international boundary reads "Children of a common mother"; on the Canadian side, "Brethren dwelling together in unity"; and on the iron gate inside the arch, "May these gates never close." Those words brought me to tears as we passed.

I crossed the border as Evelyn Kaganowicz, but shortly afterwards Leon and I changed our last name to a surname that was not so foreign and was easier to pronounce. We chose Kahn, the surname of one of his cousins in San Francisco.

I already had many names for what felt like many lives when I landed in Vancouver. Ewa Landsman, Howa Krawa, Eva Krawa, Howa Schuster, Evelyn Landsman and Evelyn Kaganowicz.

I now had one more. Evelyn Kahn. A new name for a new life. My future would belong to her.

Epilogue

I am the only one left to chronicle the lives of Hoda, Basia, Rivke and Joe. These are their final chapters.

HODA

COURTESY OF EVELYN KAHN

Hoda lived a simple life in America. She managed the household and took care of her family. Hoda never mastered English, as there was no need. She lived in a little self-contained Yiddish-speaking world in the Bronx. Her friends were other survivors with whom she would get together for a stroll or an afternoon of cards. It was hard when her family began to leave the nest. She was able to visit Rivke and Joe in New Jersey, but not Evelyn who was too far away in Vancouver. Hoda was able to meet two great-grandchildren, Mark and Charlene, when Evelyn came to visit.

Hoda Schuster passed away on December 2, 1958, while visiting Rivke. Death came quickly to Hoda. Rivke heard a strange noise in the living room, where she had made a bed for her mother so she would not have to climb the steep narrow staircase that led to the upper bedroom where Hoda usually stayed when she visited. When Rivke came into the room, she heard Hoda call out from her bed "Meishele" (a diminutive of Moshe, her great-grandson Mark's Hebrew name.) It was the last utterance on her lips before she took her final breath. Bobe Hoda was seventy-two years old. She is buried in the Eishishok Society section of the United Hebrew Cemetery on Staten Island.

COURTESY OF EVELYN KAHN

BASIA

Basia remained in the Bronx for several years after Hoda's passing and worked in a ladies clothing factory in the garment district in Manhattan making snowsuits for children. In 1965, she moved to Vancouver and lived in an apartment a short walk from her family. Basia loved spoiling her grandchildren, especially having them over for sleepovers and teaching them card games. She developed a circle of friends with whom she socialized. Her coin purse was always full and at the ready for her weekly card games with "the ladies." Basia enjoyed walking, baking, going out for lunch and window shopping.

The retinitis pigmentosa that had presented itself with the episode of night blindness when we escaped from the ghetto to the forest progressively robbed Basia of her peripheral vision, reducing her sight to almost nothing. It nearly cost her her life. As she was cooking one evening, a kitchen towel next to the burner on the stove caught fire and caused third-degree burns to Basia's face and chest. It is a measure of her fortitude that she managed to call Evelyn and her granddaughter, Hodie, who rushed to Basia's apartment. Basia, not comprehending the severity of her injuries, had already begun treating them by applying burn cream to her skin. However, these burns were far beyond a salve. It was clear she needed emergency care. She was rushed by ambulance to the hospital. Of all the injuries Basia suffered, there is no question the recovery from those burns was the most painful for her but not, unfortunately, the only pain she was destined to endure.

Bessie, Bronx, 1954.
COURTESY OF EVELYN KAHN

The abscess on Basia's leg as a result of the thrombosis during childbirth was a constant source of discomfort and potential infection.

Basia tended to the wound with meticulous daily care. It is nothing short of miraculous that she managed to keep it from becoming infected, especially during the two years spent in the forest. Unfortunately, Basia had not counted on developing diabetes in middle age. Although she was scrupulous about her diet, the ravages of the disease on her leg would prove devastating. The ulcer had damaged too much tissue. Basia's leg had to be amputated, another blow in a lifetime of cruel blows.

Basia worked like a lioness at GF Strong Rehabilitation Centre, in Vancouver, for nine long months to be fitted with a prosthetic leg. All the health professionals there were deeply moved by the mental strength and great courage of their seventy-six-year-old patient and by her fierce commitment to go on with life in spite of her difficult circumstances. Her grit and determination paid off.

Bessie, walking down the aisle at Mark's wedding, escorted by Hodie, Phoenix, AZ, 1985.
COURTESY OF EVELYN KAHN

One year later, on February 17, 1985, Basia walked down the aisle at her grandson Mark's wedding, escorted by Hodie. Ever the lover of textiles, Basia had saved some royal blue–flecked, velvet chiffon fabric she had originally intended for a dress for Mark's bar mitzvah in 1968. Instead she used it for a gown for his wedding. Basia's vision was nearly completely gone by then but she wanted to know what she looked like. Evelyn described every detail of the dress to her: where the bodice was, the length, the draping, the form. Basia looked like a dowager queen, regal and serene. An approving smile formed on Basia's lips, radiating across her face.

Basia Landsman passed away on March 8, 1985, barely a month after Mark's wedding. She was seventy-seven years old. She is buried in Schara Tzedeck Cemetery, in New Westminster, BC. On New Year's day 1986, ten months after she was laid to rest, Basia's name passed to her first great-grandchild, Danielle Batya.

COURTESY OF EVELYN KAHN

RIVKE

In 1950, Rivke and her husband, Melach, moved to Melach's chicken farm in Freehold, New Jersey. It was there that Rivke built a new life for her and Joe, then age seven. Freehold was home to a sizable, flourishing community of Eastern European Jews, including Holocaust survivors, who had been assisted by Jewish aid agencies with crucial loans to help them get established. The community was close-knit and Rivke found her place among the other new immigrants, especially the chicken farmers. They socialized together and helped one another.

Rivke and Joe, Lakewood, NJ, 1954.
COURTESY OF EVELYN KAHN

Chicken farming was not hard to learn, but it was hard to do. Rivke was a quick learner and was soon immersed in the rhythms of her chickens, rising early to feed them and collect eggs. She had a natural affinity for animals and enjoyed several dogs and cats on the farm.

In the late 1960s, Rivke bought a shoe store, possibly in response to a decline at the time in the poultry industry in the area. The store would eventually fail, but thankfully the farm provided enough sustenance for her and Joe. By then, Melach had moved to a long-term care home.

On January 2, 1986, Rivke suffered a fatal heart attack in her doctor's office, right after telling Joe "Heint gey ich shtarben (Today I am going to die)." She was sixty-five years old.

Two days later, according to the wish she expressed during her lifetime, Rivke was laid to rest next to her mother, Hoda, in the Eishishok Society section of the United Hebrew Cemetery on Staten Island.

COURTESY OF EVELYN KAHN

JOE

In 1956, at age thirteen, Joe moved back to the Bronx to live with his aunt Basia and grandmother Hoda so he could attend Yeshiva University High School in Washington Heights. It was a time of much optimism for him. He was a handsome, bright, sweet-tempered teen. At his bar mitzvah (a coming-of-age ritual for Jewish males) that year, Joe was a strapping 5 feet, 8 inches tall, well on his way to his eventual full height of 6 feet, 2 inches. He confidently led the entire synagogue service and delivered a beautiful bar mitzvah speech. He praised and gave thanks to Rivke and Basia and even found words of kindness for his stepfather. But his highest praise was for Bobe Hoda, whom he thanked for saving him from death in the forest.

When Joe was around age fifteen, Hoda had her first heart attack. Joe thought she was dying. His grandmother was Joe's rock and his mainstay. The trauma of her illness was a breaking point for him. It triggered a bout of severe depression, the first of many episodes over the following years. At age seventeen, Joe was diagnosed with schizophrenia. He would struggle for the rest of his life with the trials of his mental illness.

Joe moved back to New Jersey after high school and started an internship as a print setter. He became very proficient, but the noisy mechanical humming and pounding rhythms of the machines were hard for him to endure. He struggled to show up for work and was eventually let go. He moved on to become a salesman in a shoe store his mother bought, in part to provide Joe with employment and keep him occupied. He enjoyed his work. He was friendly and curious about people. He was a savant on the subject of U.S. presidents and he loved to question his customers—and anyone he met—about presidential birthdates. The store was ultimately not successful and eventually had to be sold.

A little time after Joe began at the shoe store, his mother contacted a Jewish matchmaker to find her son a match. The chosen bride was Varda Scheinberg, from Ramat Gan, Israel, a suburb of Tel Aviv. A year after the wedding, Joe became a father.

Standing (l-r): Rivke, Sammy, Joe, Evelyn, and Leon at Sammy's bar mitzvah, Tel Aviv, Israel, 1983.
COURTESY OF SAMMY JOSELEWITZ

Seated (l-r): Sammy, Patti, Eleeza and Eitan Joselewitz, Tel Aviv, 2022.
COURTESY OF SAMMY JOSELEWITZ

Unfortunately, married life would prove to be too challenging for the couple, and when their son was age three, Varda returned to Israel to raise him with her family.

After his mother's passing, Joe moved to Vancouver to live briefly with Evelyn, but the arrangement was not sustainable. His needs were complex. He moved to the Louis Brier Home and Hospital, a Jewish care home for seniors, where he remained for the rest of his life. Joe passed away on November 23, 2020. He had endured a lifetime of challenges, beginning with his birth, but he will be forever remembered by his cousins and through his beautiful legacy—Sammy, his wife Patti, and Joe's two grandchildren, Eleeza and Eitan. Joe is buried at the Schara Tzedeck Cemetery, in New Westminster, BC.

Evelyn, informal graduation photo, Bronx, NY, 1952.
COURTESY OF EVELYN KAHN

EVELYN

Evelyn's first impression of Vancouver was that it was undeniably beautiful, but felt like a shtetl compared to New York—quiet, provincial and slow-paced. She missed the energy and sophistication of the big metropolis she had left and initially found the other newcomers dull. Over time, she adjusted to her new surroundings, gradually building friendships, finding her community and creating a fulfilling life as a devoted wife, loving mother and capable homemaker.

In her early days, Evelyn tackled the steep learning curve of 1950s domestic life. Having never lived on her own, she had to learn how to cook, clean, shop and manage a household—all far from the support system she had known. With determination and creativity, she turned Leon's sparse bachelor pad into a cozy, welcoming home. She painted walls, laid new linoleum flooring and sewed curtain panels from fabric remnants. Her cooking, initially limited to burning dry macaroni in a frying pan, evolved into a talent for preparing elegant meals and hosting refined dinner parties.

Evelyn's social circle formed around the wives of Leon's fellow Holocaust survivor friends. On modest budgets, the couples entertained in each other's homes—card games for the men, conversation for the women. Evelyn also loved the rare night out dancing and dining.

In 1954, Evelyn gave birth to her first child, Mark. When the toddler developed a habit of tossing his glass milk bottles on the floor of their appartment creating a constant noise hazard for their downstair's neighbour—the family was evicted from their apartment. Scraping together a modest downpayment, they managed to buy a small split-level house. Three more children followed in quick succession. By September 1960, Evelyn was thriving in her role as a busy mother of four children under the age of six.

But Evelyn's strength was soon tested by her first daughter, Charlene. Almost immediately after her birth, Evelyn sensed that something was not right. After consultations with pediatricians and specialists in Vancouver and New York, she received devastating news: Charlene had profound cognitive and physical impairments. She would never develop normally. Eventually diagnosed with microcephaly, Charlene began to suffer from seizures and her care became increasingly demanding. As Evelyn tended to Charlene's growing needs, two more babies arrived—Hodie and Saul. The load became too much. With heavy hearts, Evelyn and Leon made the painful decision to place Charlene in Woodlands School, a residential facility for children with severe disabilities. Visiting her was emotionally wrenching for Evelyn. Her beloved Charlene passed away at the age of nine, in 1966.

Though Evelyn never stopped grieving her daughter, she remained deeply grateful for her three healthy children.

After Charlene's death, Evelyn slowly reclaimed parts of herself. She rekindled her aesthetic passions—devouring magazines on architecture, decor, visual arts and fashion. Her hobby became a profession when Block Bros., a leading real estate developer, hired her to design lobbies in their new apartment buildings. One was even featured in a 1967 issue of *Vancouver Magazine*.

She also returned to singing, joining the Jewish Community Centre Choir and performing as a featured soloist. Deeply engaged in Jewish communal life, she organized fundraisers and hosted visiting dignitaries in her home, including Simon Wiesenthal, Menachem Begin and Natan Sharansky. She proudly helped establish Yaffa House, a group home for Jewish adults with mental health challenges. Her home was always open to guests, and it became a hub of Jewish hospitality.

Evelyn excelled as a hostess, combining flair with unshakable composure. On one memorable evening, she accidentally reversed her car through her own fence, landing the auto on its side in her neighbour's driveway. After being rescued and cleared by emergency services, she calmly returned to her home, revived her wilted canapés and received her guests with a smile—and a great story to share over cocktails.

Eager to see first-hand the cultures and designs featured in the magazines she read, Evelyn began to travel. She visited more frequently with her old survivor friends in New York, including Mike and Darlene Alpert, Ben and Ruth Koren, and Masha Seiden. She built friendships around the world, especially in Florida and Mexico City, and embraced travel as a form of continuing education and enrichment.

Evelyn and Leon Kahn, Vancouver, BC, 1987.
COURTESY OF EVELYN KAHN

In 2003, Evelyn's life changed again with the sudden death of Leon. Just two weeks earlier, they had celebrated their fiftieth wedding anniversary in New York. Evelyn was scheduled to return to Vancouver a few days after Leon and was still in New York when he died. The shock was profound, and she was overwhelmed with grief. It took time, but she emerged from that darkness with new resolve.

For the first time, Evelyn became the sole decision-maker in her life. She built a new home—one she had dreamed of designing with Leon—and poured her energy into getting every detail right. She bought and renovated a condo in Florida, where she nurtured wonderful new friendships with members of Miami's large Latin American Jewish community, especially Perla Gilinski and her family, who warmly embraced Evelyn and made her one of their own.

Reflecting on her life, Evelyn sees a journey marked by resilience and reinvention. She came to Canada as a young bride and built a rich life alongside her husband. After widowhood, she built another—this time as an independent woman.

I am a mother, grandmother and great grandmother. And I will always be a survivor.

Acknowledgements

This memoir has been a labour of love and a long journey of intention interrupted by life. To all who joined me along the way, thank you for helping me bring my memoir to life.

My deepest gratitude to my dear friend, Mike Alpert, who supported me by patiently answering my endless questions to clarify and affirm my recollections of our shared history.

Thank you to the survivors whose invaluable Holocaust memoirs inspired me and enhanced my understanding of events I was too young at the time to fully comprehend. Your stories are a precious gift.

Special thanks to the many others who played roles, small to large, in providing supplemental details and invaluable assistance with research, fact-checking, tracking down archival records, and filling in the blanks and substance of my history. Cousin Judy Baston and Russ Maurer of the indispensable Lithuanian genealogy resource, LitvakSIG; Shaun Goldstone of the JDC; Bernard Pinsky and Max Pinsky; Tamara Vershitskaya, founder of the Jewish Resistance Museum in Novogrudok; and the wonderful team at the Vancouver Holocaust Education Center—Nina Krieger, Ilona Schulman-Spear, Tessa Coutu, Caitlin Donaldson, and Chase Nelson.

Barbi Braude, there are not enough words to express my gratitude to you for sharing your creative vision and talents, bringing form and beauty to my memoir. It is everything I hoped for—and more.

My thanks to my wonderful publisher Wendy Atkinson at Ronsdale, and her amazing team—Kevin Welsh, Kelly Laycock, and "memoir whisperer" Robyn So. Thank you for embracing my story and for your unwavering support, generosity, encouragement, eagle eyes—and patience—in guiding a first-time author through her debut writing effort.

My most profound and heartfelt gratitude to my very special daughter, Hodie, my Hodele, aptly named for my bobe. Thank you for helping me realize my dream of writing my Holocaust story. I am filled with pride for how you lovingly and determinedly turned my raw handwritten recollections into a fluent and authentic narrative—all while staying true to my voice. Because of your persistence in confirming and digging for facts, you also enabled me to learn things I never knew—including names of long-lost family members and details about the lives of others. I have cherished working with you. I will forever treasure the moments that brought us to happy tears—not sad ones—like when we laughed together as I taught you Russian or how to pronounce Yiddish words like a proper Litvak. Remember: ניין is pronounced *neyn*, not "nine."

My sincere apologies to anyone I may have inadvertently omitted or misquoted and for any other errors—factual or otherwise. Writing a memoir in your ninth decade has its limitations.

Further Reading

Brysk, Miriam M.
Amidst the Shadows of Trees.
Yellow Start, 2007.

The personal story of a young girl's survival in the Holocaust, hiding with partisans in the Lipichanska forest of Belarus.

Eliach, Yaffa.
There Once Was a World: A 900-Year Chronicle of the Shtetl of Eishyshok.
Back Bay Books, 1999.

A monumental chronicle of Jewish life in the Lithuanian shtetl of Eishyshok, tracing its nine-hundred-year history and destruction in the Holocaust.

Frankel, Rebecca.
Into the Forest: A Holocaust Story of Survival, Triumph, and Love.
St. Martin's Griffin, 2021.

The inspiring journey of a family's flight from Nazi persecution into the deep forests of Belarus.

Kahn, Leon.
No Time to Mourn: The True Story of a Jewish Partisan Fighter.
Ronsdale Press, 2004.

A firsthand account of a Jewish teen's survival and vengeance in the forests of Nazi-occupied Lithuania.

Levine, Allan.
Fugitives of the Forest.
Stoddart Publishing, 1998.

A historical account of Jewish resistance during World War II, highlighting partisan groups across Poland, Belarus and Lithuania.

Minuskin, Kalman.
In the Ghetto and in the Forest.
The Color Factor, 2014.

A memoir recounting the author's experiences in a Belorussian ghetto and later as a Jewish partisan fighting in the forests of Belarus.

Pinsky, Bernard.
Ordinary Extraordinary: My Father's Life.
Behind the Book, 2023.

A son's moving tribute to his father, Rubin Pinsky—a Holocaust survivor and Jewish partisan who rebuilt his life in Canada after the war.

Glossary of Foreign Terms

This glossary provides definitions for foreign terms used in this memoir. Pronunciations are given in a simplified phonetic style with stressed syllables **bolded**.

afikomen (a-fee-**koh**-men, Hebrew): Half a matzoh, hidden during the Seder, and once found, served at the end of the Passover dinner. Derived from the Greek word *epikomon*, meaning "dessert" or "after dinner revelry."

aliyah (**ah**-lee-yah, Hebrew): Literally "ascent" or "rise." The immigration of Jews to the Land of Israel.

aron kodesh (**ah**-ron **koh**-desh, Hebrew): Holy ark; houses the Torah scrolls in a synagogue.

ayin hara (ah-yin hah-**rah**, Hebrew): "The evil eye." Jewish concept of the harmful effects of jealousy and envy.

bankes (**bahn**-kes, Yiddish): Cupping, a traditional Jewish healing remedy, similar in practice to Chinese medicine techniques to cleanse the body of toxins.

becker (**bek**-er, Yiddish): Baker.

benching licht (**bench**-ing likht, Yiddish): "Blessing the lights." The ritual act of lighting Jewish Sabbath and festival candles.

bendl (**ben**-dl, Yiddish): A red-coloured string believed to protect the wearer from the evil eye.

bimah (bee-mah, Hebrew): A raised platform in the synagogue from where the Torah is read and services are led.

birkat hamazon (**beer-kat** ha-mazon, Hebrew): grace after meals.

blatt (blaht, Yiddish): The front and back of a single page of Gemara.

blekher (**blekh**-er, Yiddish): Sheet metal worker.

bohnenkaffee (boh-nen-**kah**-fey, German): "Bean coffee." A coffee shop serving this type of coffee.

Bricha (**bree**-khah, Hebrew): Jewish underground movement that helped Holocaust survivors reach the west and Palestine.

challah (**khah**-lah, Hebrew): Traditional braided bread served on Sabbath and festivals.

chametz (**khah**-metz, Hebrew): Leavened food, forbidden on Passover.

chazzan (khah-**zahn**, Hebrew): Cantor; a synagogue prayer leader.

chevra kadisha (**khev**-rah kah-**dee**-shah, Hebrew): Jewish burial society.

cholent (**cho**-lent, Yiddish): Hearty slow-cooked meat and potato stew, traditionally eaten on the Sabbath.

Chumash (khoo-**mahsh**, Hebrew): An acronym derived from the word for "five," referring to the Torah, the first "five books of Moses": Genesis, Exodus, Leviticus, Numbers, and Deuteronomy.

churban (**khoor**-bahn, Hebrew): Total destruction.

dacha (**dah**-chah, Russian): A little weekend cottage or country house.

Diaspora (dye-**as**-poh-rah, English): Jews living outside Israel.

din Torah (**dean** To-rah, Hebrew): A Jewish court proceeding or ruling.

doragaya dochka (doh-rah-**gah**-yah **doch**-kah, Russian): Darling daughter.

dubl (**doo**-bl, Yiddish): "Double." Commonly found in Eastern European homes, a small hinged ventilation window set within a larger window that can be opened independently to allow fresh air without fully opening the main window.

Endlösung der Judenfrage (**ent-loh-zoong dare yoo**-den-fra-geh, German): "Final Solution to the Jewish Question," the Nazi regime's term for its plan exterminate the Jewish people.

felsher (**fel**-sher, Yiddish): A practitioner of holistic medicine.

gaon (gah-**ohn**, Hebrew): A genius. An honorific used for great rabbinic authorities, often combined with their city of residence, e.g. the Vilna Gaon.

gardine (**gahr**-deen-eh, Yiddish): Curtains, especially sheer or decorative window treatments.

garmon (**gahr**-mon, Russian): A small Russian accordion.

gefilte (geh-**fil**-teh, Yiddish): Stuffed fish, commonly referring to gefilte fish.

Gemara (geh-**mah**-rah, Hebrew): Rabbinic analyses, deliberations, and commentaries on the Mishna (second-century compilation of Jewish oral law) that came into its final collected form in the sixth or seventh century and which forms the foundation of normative Jewish law today.

goldene medina (**gol**-de-neh meh-**dee**-nah, Yiddish): The "golden land." Refers to America.

Haggadah (hah-**gah**-dah, Hebrew): The book used to guide the Passover Seder; includes songs, stories, rituals, and prayers to tell the story of the Jewish Exodus from slavery in Egypt to freedom.

hamentashen (**hah**-men-**tah**-shen, Yiddish): A triangular-shaped pastry eaten on the Jewish holiday of Purim, stuffed with traditional fillings of apricot, prune, or poppy seed. The pastry's name is derived from the words "Haman" (the villain in the Purim story) and "tashe" (meaning "pocket" or "pouch"). The shape of the pastry is meant to resemble Haman's hat or his ears.

Hashem (hah-**shem**, Hebrew): "The Name." A respectful term used by Jews to refer to God.

High Holy Days (high hoh-lee dayz, English): Rosh Hashanah (Jewish New Year) and Yom Kippur (Day of Atonement), the most solemn days of the Jewish year. They are bookends of a ten-day period of self-reflection and spiritual cleansing, collectively known in Hebrew as the Yamim Noraim (Days of Awe).

hopak (**hoh**-pahk, Ukrainian): Ukrainian folk dance.

Judenrat (**yoo**-den-raht, German): Jewish Council tasked with implementing and enforcing Nazi orders in Jewish communities during the Second World War. The plural form is Judenräte.

Kaddish (**kah**-dish, Hebrew): Jewish prayer recited in memory of the dead, chanted from the day of burial for thirty days and up to eleven months, depending on the degree of the family relationship, and annually on the yahrzeit (anniversary of passing).

kahal (**kah**-hahl, Hebrew): Municipal governing authority, historically referring to Jewish community governance.

kamerton (**kah**-mer-ton, Russian): Two-pronged tuning fork, used by cantors to ensure the correct musical pitch for liturgy and prayers.

kaparot (kah-**pah**-roht, Hebrew): Ritual of atonement that is said on the eve of Yom Kippur.

kashehs (**kash**-ehs, Yiddish): Questions.

kashke marilke (**kash**-keh mah-**ril**-keh, Yiddish): A rich sauce-like concoction, similar to a chocolate ganache.

kashrut (**kahsh**-root, Hebrew): Jewish dietary laws (kosher laws).

katukh (kah-**tookh**, Yiddish): Small hollow space underneath a counter.

keppel (**kep**-el, Yiddish): Stiff cantorial cap.

kessel (**kes**-el, Yiddish): Large metal barrel used to boil water for household needs.

kichelach (**khee**-khel-akh, Yiddish): Dry, airy bowtie-shaped cookies, sprinkled with sugar.

kiddush (kee-**doosh**, Hebrew): Ritual blessing over wine, often recited on Sabbath and festivals.

kippah (**kip**-ah, Hebrew): Skull cap worn by Jewish males.

kishke (**kish**-keh, Yiddish): Stuffed cow intestine (a type of sausage).

kneipe (**knigh**-peh, German): Pub or tavern.

kneydlakh (**kney**-dlakh, Yiddish): Matzoh balls, round dumplings traditionally served in chicken soup, particularly at Passover. Made from matzoh meal, beaten eggs, water, and a fat (such as shmaltz), the dumplings can be light and fluffy or dense and chewy.

kochleffel (**kokh**-lef-el, German/Yiddish): Wooden cooking spoon. Yiddish colloquialism for a "pot stirrer," an overbearing person who meddles or interferes in matters that do not concern them.

krawa (**krah**-vah, Polish): Cow.

kremlach (**krem**-lakh, Yiddish): Small shops, plural of *kremel.*

kreplach (**krep**-lakh, Yiddish): Little dumplings of very fine dough stuffed with ground beef.

kuchnya (**kookh**-nyah, Russian): Field kitchen used by the Soviet army.

kugele (**koo**-geh-leh, Yiddish): Small baked pudding from starch (noodles or potatoes), eggs, and fat; often sweet.

kvetchen dem benkel (**kvet**-chen dem **ben-kel**, Yiddish): "Wear down the little bench," an idiom to describe someone glued to his bottom studying (religious texts) all day, instead of working or engaging in more worldly affairs.

Lebensraum (**lay**-bens-rowm, **German**): Living space.

liquidation (English): The forced emptying and destruction of Jewish ghettos, towns, and communities through violent roundups, deportation, and mass murder (contextual to the Holocaust).

lokshen (lokh-shen, Yiddish): Egg noodles.

Ma Nishtanah (mah nish-tah-**nah**, Hebrew): Prayer recited at the Passover Seder (ritual meal), typically sung by the youngest child present, enquiring about key differences between Passover and regular Jewish meals.

madrichim (mah-dree-**kheem**, Hebrew): Male counsellors or youth leaders, especially in Jewish camps, youth movements, and educational programs. Plural of madrich.

matzoh (maht-zoh, Hebrew): Unleavened flat bread eaten on Passover, made from flour and water and baked quickly to prevent leavening.

matzoh meal (maht-zoh meel, Hebrew/English): Finely ground matzoh, used on Passover as a substitute for flour or breadcrumbs.

mikvah (mik-vah, Hebrew): A ritual bath filled with water from natural sources sanctioned by Jewish law—such as rainwater or spring water—used in Jewish practice for spiritual purification of the body and utensils.

mischlinge (mish **ling**-eh, German): The legal term used by the Nazis to denote those with mixed Aryan and Jewish ancestry.

Modeh Ani (moh-**deh** a-**nee**, Hebrew): "I Give Thanks." A short Jewish prayer said upon waking, thanking God for returning one's soul after the "minor death" of sleep.

negel vasser (neg-el **vah**-ser, Yiddish): "Nail water." A hand-rinsing ritual performed upon waking in the morning to rinse the hands of spiritual impurities.

neshama (ne-shah-**mah**, Hebrew): Soul.

oblava (ob-**lah**-vah, Russian): Manhunt; raid; round-up; systematic search operations targeting hidden Jews and partisans in the forests by German troops and local collaborators (Lithuanian, Ukrainian, or Belorussian auxiliaries).

Olam Haba (oh-lahm hah-**bah**, Hebrew): The "World to Come." Heaven; the afterlife.

Oneg Shabbat (oh-neg shah-**baht**, Hebrew): "Joy" or "Delight" of the Sabbath. A social gathering with singing, food, Torah discussion, and fellowship traditionally held on Friday night to welcome the Sabbath.

otriad (ot-**ryahd**, Russian): A partisan unit or military group.

pirozhki (pee-**rozh**-kee, Russian): Little hand-pies, baked or fried, and filled with savory or sweet fillings.

podryat (pod-**ryat**, Russian): Continuous communal effort, as in an assembly line.

podstakan (pod-**stah**-kahn, Russian): "Under the glass." A traditional Russian metal glass holder, used for tea to allow one to drink without burning one's fingers.

pogrom (poh-**grom**, Russian): Destroy; wreak havoc. A violent mob attack against ethnic minorities—especially Jews—often with the tacit approval of local authorities, and marked by looting, destruction of property, physical violence, and, often, murder.

Pomaháye Boh (poh-mah-**hah**-yeh boh, Ukrainian): "May God help (your bounty)."

poziomki (poh-**zyom**-kee, Polish): Small, wild, aromatic forest strawberries.

ptcha (ptchah, Yiddish): Jellied calf's feet.

Purim (poo-rim, Hebrew): A joyful holiday marked by costumes, charity, feasts and public readings of the Book of Esther, the story of the salvation of the Jewish people from annihilation in ancient Persia. Purim is the plural for the word "lots," which were cast by the king of Persia's vizier, Haman, to determine the date for the planned massacre.

puszcza (poosh-chah, Polish): Primeval forest, ancient woodland; an expansive, largely untouched landscape. The plural form is *puszcze*.

rad kromen (rahd-kromen, Yiddish): A small strip of shops set side by side in a market square.

sabbotnik (sah-**bot**-neek, Russian): A gentile hired to do certain chores on Shabbat that are prohibited to Jews. Derived from the word "Shabbat."

scheinen (**shy**-nen, German): Official-looking Nazi documents or passes, sometimes issued by organizations such as the Jewish Councils (Judenräte) as a way to control and manage Jews while giving the illusion of safety or legitimacy. Often given to individuals deemed to have skills useful to the Nazis with the pretense of affording the holder legal status or protection.

seder (seh-der, Hebrew): Ritual "ordered" Passover evening meal, choreographed by the Haggadah, designed to commemorate the Exodus—the Jewish journey from slavery in Egypt to freedom—using symbolic foods, storytelling, songs, and prayers.

semejnaja gruppa (se-mey-**nah**-yah groo-pah, Russian): Family group.

semicha (se-**mee**-khah, Hebrew): Rabbinical ordination.

Shabbat (shah-**baht**, Hebrew): Sabbath; the day of rest in Judaism.

shamas (**shah**-mahss, Yiddish): Sexton, the employee responsible for the maintenance and upkeep of a synagogue.

sharvens (**shar**-vens, Yiddish): Clay shards placed on the eyes and mouth of the deceased as part of the tahara (Jewish ritual preparation of the body for burial).

Shema (sheh-**mah**, Hebrew): The bedtime prayer recited before going to sleep. It expresses faith and protection and includes parts of the longer *Shema Yisrael* (Hear, O Israel) prayer, which is central to Jewish life.

shepped naches (**shep**-ed **nah**-khes, Yiddish): Beamed with pride; took pleasure; derived joy.

shidduch (**shi**-dookh, Yiddish): Matching a couple; arranging a marriage.

shisel (**shi**-sel, Yiddish): A small container or dish used to cook or serve food.

shmaltz (shmaltzz, Yiddish): Poultry fat.

Shoah (**shoh**-ah, Hebrew): Holocaust.

shochet (**shoh**-khet, Yiddish): Ritual Jewish slaughterer, who performs kosher slaughter.

shpatziren (shpah-**tzee**-ren, Yiddish): A leisurely stroll or walk.

shtetl (**shtet**-l, Yiddish): Small town, historically referring to a Jewish town or village in Eastern Europe.

shul (shool, Yiddish): Synagogue.

skhron (skhron, Russian): Dugout; a secret or underground place where something is stored or concealed.

skwarski (**skvar**-skee, Polish): Crispy bits of fried lard.

tachrichim (tah-khree-**kheem**, Hebrew): Traditional white linen Jewish burial shrouds.

tahara (tah-hah-**rah**, Hebrew): Jewish ritual purification of the body for burial.

tallit (tah-**leet**, Hebrew): Jewish prayer shawl, traditionally worn during morning prayers. It is distinguished by four fringes (tzitzit) at its corners, as commanded in Numbers 15:38–39.

tefillin (tef-i-**lin**, Hebrew): Phylacteries, a set of two small black leather boxes containing small scrolls of parchment inscribed with specific verses from the Torah, worn by Jewish men during weekday morning prayers.

tehillim (teh-hi-**leem**, Hebrew): The Book of Psalms; songs of praise from the book.

tenaim (teh-**nah**-eem, Hebrew): Terms of the betrothal; this ritual is usually observed at the groom's reception (tish), when the wedding contract is also signed and witnessed.

tichel (**ti**-khel, Yiddish): A headscarf worn by Orthodox married women in accordance with Jewish laws of modesty.

traif (**tray**-f, Yiddish): Non-kosher food.

tserkva (**tser**-kvah, Russian): Russian/Ukrainian Orthodox church building or place of worship.

tzadekes (tsah-**deh**-kes, Yiddish): A righteous person. (Feminine form of *tzaddik*.)

tzimmes (**tsi**-mes, Yiddish): Sweet stewed carrots, often made with dried fruits, such as prunes.

va'ad (**vah**-ahd, Hebrew): Jewish community council.

vekhslakh (**vekhs**-lakh, Yiddish): Credit slips.

Viddui (vee-**doo**-ee, Hebrew): Confession; a short prayer recited on Yom Kippur, and before one departs from this world.

Volksdeutsche (**folks**-doy-che, German): An ethnic German born or living outside Germany who did not hold German citizenship.

Volkskörper (**folks**-kur-per, German): German national body.

Volksschule (**folks**-shoo-leh, German): A small elementary school for young children.

wieczerza (vyeh-**cheh**-rzah, Polish): The evening meal; supper.

yahrzeit (**yahr**-tzite, Yiddish): Anniversary of the passing of a loved one.

z"l (zahl, Hebrew): Abbreviation for a post-nominal honorific, *zichrono livracha* (masc.) or *zichrona livracha* (fem.), meaning "of blessed memory."

zaftig (**zahf**-tig, Yiddish): Juicy; plump; curvy; well-rounded; full-bodied.

zemlyanka (zem-**lyan**-kah, Russian): Earth house; crude underground shelter.

zmirot (zmee-**roht**, Hebrew): Shabbat songs, often sung at Friday night and Saturday daytime meals.

zt"l (zahtz-l, Hebrew): Abbreviation for a post-nominal honorific for a scholar or sage, *zecher tzaddik livracha*, meaning "May the memory of the righteous one be a blessing."

Geographic Names and Regional Spellings

This reference table includes all the geographic names mentioned, with corresponding regional variations and spellings by country. For example, Eishyshok was always the Yiddish name, but when it was part of Poland it was known as Ejszyszki and is now Eišiškės, Lithuania.

PRESENT-DAY LOCATION	YIDDISH (TRANSLATED)	BELARUSIAN	ENGLISH
Lithuania	Eishyshok	Эйшышкі (Eishyshki)	Eishishok
Belarus	Kurpyash	Курпяшы (Kurpyashy)	Kurpyashy
Belarus	Lida	Ліда (Lida)	Lida
Poland	Lodzh	Лодзь (Łódź)	Łódź
Belarus	Ludzich	Людзічы (Liudzichy)	Ludzichy
Belarus	Nakrishok	Накрышкі (Nakryshki)	Nakryshki
Lithuania	Podbrodze	Падбраддзе (Padbraddzie)	Podbrodzie
Lithuania	Pumpyan	Пумпяны (Pumpiany)	Pumpiany
Belarus	Puszcza Lipichanska	Ліпічанская пушча (Lipichanskaya Pushcha)	Lipichany Forest
Belarus	Puszcza Naliboki	Налібоцкая пушча (Nalibotskaya Pushcha)	Naliboki Forest
Lithuania	Vilna	Вільня (Vilnya)	Vilnius
Belarus	Zhetel	Дзятлава (Dzyatlava)	Dzyatlava

The names of the shtetls, towns and forests mentioned in this memoir were transliterated from the Yiddish names by which they were known to the author and her community during the time period covered in this book.

LITHUANIAN	POLISH	RUSSIAN	YIDDISH
Eišiškės	Ejszyszki	Эйшишки (Eishishki)	אײשישאָק
Kurpiškės	Kurpiasz	Курпяшы (Kurpyashy)	קערפּיאַש
Lyda	Lida	Лида (Lida)	לידע
Lodzė	Łódź	Лодзь (Łódź)	לאָדזש
Liudzičiai	Ludzice	Людичи (Lyudichi)	לודזיץ
Nėkriškiai	Nakryszki	Накрышкi (Nakryshki)	נאַקרישאָק
Pabradė	Podbrodzie	Подбродье (Podbrodye)	פּאָדבראָדזע
Pumpėnai	Pumpiany	Пумпяны (Pumpiany)	פּומפּיאַן
Lipičansko giria	Puszcza Lipiczańska	Липичанская пуща (Lipichanskaya Pushcha)	ליפּיטשאַנער װאַלד
Nalibokų giria	Puszcza Nalibocka	Налибокская пуща (Nalibokskaya Pushcha)	נאַליבאָקער װאַלד
Vilnius	Wilno	Вильнюс (Vilnyus)	װילנע
Zietela	Zdzięcioł	Дятлово (Dyatlovo)	זשעטל

The Authors

Evelyn Kahn was born in Vilna—then part of Poland—in 1933. She immigrated to Canada in 1953 with her husband, Leon *z"l*, a fellow Holocaust survivor and former partisan fighter. Together, they rebuilt their lives and raised a beautiful family. Evelyn lives in Vancouver, along with her three children—Mark, Hodie, and Saul. Now in her ninth decade, she cherishes every moment with her grandchildren and great-grandchildren—scattered nearby and across the world—each one a living testament to her survival, courage, enduring spirit, and good fortune.

Hodie Kahn is the daughter of Evelyn and the late Leon Kahn z"l. As the child of two Holocaust survivors, she considers it a sacred inheritance to carry their memory forward. Working closely with her mother to shape this memoir has been both a personal and educational journey, and an act of devotion. She is grateful to help preserve this story of survival, strength, and love—a legacy for her own children, her brothers and their families, and for generations to come. Hodie divides her time between Vancouver and Israel, holding both places close to her heart.